To my dad, Joe Foy

Theresa Foy DiGeronimo, M.Ed.

How to **Talk to Your Senior Parents** About **Really Important Things**

Specific Questions and Answers and Useful Things to Say

JOSSEY-BASS
A Wiley Company
San Francisco

JOSSEY-BASS
A Wiley Company
350 Sansome St.
San Francisco, CA 94104-1342

www.josseybass.com

Jossey-Bass books and products are available through most bookstores. To contact Jossey-Bass directly, call (888) 378-2537, fax to (800) 605-2665, or visit our website at www.josseybass.com.

Substantial discounts on bulk quantities of Jossey-Bass books are available to corporations, professional associations, and other organizations. For details and discount information, contact the special sales department at Jossey-Bass.

We at Jossey-Bass strive to use the most environmentally sensitive paper stocks available to us. Our publications are printed on acid-free recycled stock whenever possible, and our paper always meets or exceeds minimum GPO and EPA requirements.

Library of Congress Cataloging-in-Publication Data

DiGeronimo, Theresa Foy.
    How to talk to your senior parents about really important things: specific questions and answers and useful things to say / Theresa Foy DiGeronimo. — 1st ed.
        p. cm
    ISBN 0-7879-5613-3 (alk. paper)
    1. Aging parents—United States. 2. Aging parents—United States—Family relationships. 3. Adult children of aging parents—United States. 4. Parent and adult child—United States. I. Title.
    HQ1064.U5 D54 2001
    306.874—dc21   2001002801

FIRST EDITION
PB Printing   10 9 8 7 6 5 4 3 2 1

Contents

Part Four: **Financial Issues   179**

Part Five: **End of Life   255**

Acknowledgments

I would like to acknowledge the help of my editor, Alan Rinzler, who has guided and encouraged me through each chapter. Other staff at Jossey-Bass including Adrienne Biggs, Amy Scott, and Lasell Whipple have also offered valuable assistance. I would also like to give special thanks to each of the following subject-matter experts who have willingly shared their expertise and experiences to help me make this book as up-to-date and accurate as possible:

Michael H. Beechem
Center on Aging, University of West Florida
Pensacola, Florida

David Bendix, CPA/PFS, CFP, CFS, RFC
The Bendix Financial Group
Garden City, New York

Dianne Boazman
President of the National Association of Geriatric Care Managers
Metairie, Louisiana

Carol Colleran
Hanley-Hazelden Center
West Palm Beach, Florida

Paul A. Falzone
President and CEO of The Right One
Hingham, Massachusetts

Elinor Ginzler
AARP manager of long-term care and independent living
Washington, D.C.

Angela Heath
National Association of Area Agencies on Aging
Washington, D.C.

Jane Hunley
Parkland Memorial Hospital
Dallas, Texas

Gary Katz
Wealth preservation planner
Paramus, New Jersey

Alice J. Kethley, Ph.D.
Executive director of the Benjamin Rose Institute
Cleveland, Ohio

Janice Knebl, DO
Chief of geriatrics at the University of North Texas Health Science
Center
Fort Worth, Texas

Patrick Mathiasen, M.D.
Clinical assistant professor University of Washington
Seattle, Washington

Robert Scrivano
Senior care planning consultant
Sacramento, California

Barbara Spreitzer-Berent
AgeQuest
Royal Oak, Michigan

Robert O. Weagley, Ph.D.
Associate professor of consumer and family economics at the University of Missouri-Columbia

Joe Weigel
Director of marketing and corporate communications of Hillenbrand Industries' Funeral Services Group
Batesville, Indiana

Introduction

As an adult child, you may find that talking to your parents about important things can be tricky business. Your parents are the ones who are supposed to look after your best interests and tell you what to do; you're the one who is supposed to listen and learn. But as our parents age, they are often the ones who need information and advice. This reversal of roles can be awkward and often keeps many adult children from having important conversations with their parents—and keeps many elderly parents from listening to their children. That's why this book has been written—to help you get past this awkwardness and feel free to talk to your parents and give them vital information while at the same time respecting their position as adults. In each chapter you will find a unique collection of advice, information, and sample dialogues that have been gathered from research and interviews and have been reviewed by people who are experts in many specialized fields of gerontology.

Of course, every family situation is unique. So I'd like to say right here at the start that nothing in this book should be considered gospel or the "only best way." But most suggested guidelines can be adapted to fit your family dynamics and give you a strong base from which to build open communication.

HOW TO TALK TO YOUR PARENTS

The way you talk to your parents is as important as what you say. Each chapter suggests specific guidelines appropriate for the given topic, but always keep in mind these general ground rules:

Honor Your Parent's Adulthood.   It's important that your parent maintain a sense of personal dignity. No matter how helpless your parent appears, don't talk to him as though he were a child. This can crush any remaining feelings of dignity and independence.

Don't Be Demeaning.   In our society, adults are allowed to make decisions for themselves. It is not appropriate for an adult child to take the decision-making power away from an elderly parent, even with good intentions that say, "Don't worry. I'll take care of all the details for you." As long as your parents are mentally able to make sound decisions, their wishes must be honored.

Don't Assume You Know Your Parent's Wishes.   No matter how close you are to your parent, you can't assume you know what's best or what she would want. Be careful when you hear yourself say something like, "I know my mom would much rather live in her own home than in a retirement community."

Share Ideas; Don't Dictate.   Your parents need you to share information with them; topics like estate planning, consumer fraud, and depression can be very complex and require time and effort to gather the latest facts. But your parents do not need you to tell them what to do with this information. Your goal should be to share your thoughts and then let your parents confirm, deny, or think about them—or give no comment. Scoldings, finger wagging, lectures, and arguments are counterproductive.

Be Patient and Calm.   As your parents age, they may have difficulty hearing and remembering. You may have to repeat information and clarify facts slowly. That's part of communicating with an elderly person, and it should be done without a patronizing or scolding attitude.

WHAT TO DO WHEN YOU CAN'T TALK TO YOUR PARENTS

The reality may be that you will never be able to talk to your parents about certain issues. There may be a long-standing history that prevents you from talking about your parents' finances, for example. There can be just too much emotional baggage in the way to discuss some important issues. In this case, you shouldn't turn away and avoid the topic completely; ignoring some of these "really important things" can lead to a major family crisis. If you can't be the one to step in and talk, make an effort to find someone else who can. Figure out who your parents will listen to. It might be a trusted family friend, an uncle or aunt, a member of the clergy, a physician, or your sibling. Show this person this book and explain that you think it would be a good idea if your parents had this information but that for various reasons, you're just not the one to talk about it.

There may also come a time when you can't talk to your parent because he or she suffers a physical or mental illness that makes communication impossible. In those cases, you may have to take charge and make decisions for your parent. The information in this book will show you where to turn to find the information you need. You'll find resources on such topics as dementia, geriatric care managers, alternative living arrangements, estate planning, and funeral arrangements that will point you in the right direction.

Talking to our parents can sometimes be difficult, awkward, and even frustrating, but the effort is worth it in the end. If you talk to your parents often and keep a continuous dialogue going, it won't be so difficult when one day you have to say, "Let's sit down. I want to talk about something very important." Talk often about the weather, the news, your friends and family—about anything—just keep talking. Soon you'll find that talking about the really important things will be much easier.

Why you should talk with your parents, *when* you should talk to them, and *what* you should say are what this book is all about. It strives to give you the words you'll need to talk to your parents about things that are important to their physical, emotional, and mental health and well-being.

Part One

Health and Well-Being

Activities of Daily Living

We have not been socialized to talk to our elderly parents about personal issues, but as adult children begin to do it more and more, it will become more of the norm.

Jane Hunley, MSSW, LMSW, social worker at
Parkland Memorial Hospital, Dallas, Texas

Ted's mother was getting older. He noticed it bit by bit over time in many small ways. But most telling lately was the way she took care of herself. For someone who couldn't live with a single hair out of place, she had started to look actually sloppy. Sometimes Ted would notice that her hair hadn't been washed, and her clothes often looked wrinkled or soiled. Even her fingernails were dirty the last time they met—something very unusual for someone who had been so meticulous about her appearance. But what could he say? This was really none of his business. Right?

Talking to our parents about how they live their daily lives isn't easy. They have a right to eat, bathe, and dress the way they want without interference from their children. If we start to question the way they do these things, we run the risk of insulting them. But there are situations when a simple conversation and a helping hand can make the activities of daily living much easier and safer for these loved ones.

This chapter encourages you to talk about (1) activities of daily living (ADLs), which include feeding, dressing, walking, toileting, bathing, continence, grooming, and communication, and (2) instrumental activities of daily living (IADLs), which include writing, reading, cooking, cleaning, shopping, doing laundry, climbing stairs, using the telephone, managing medication, managing money, being employed, engaging in leisure activities, and traveling. You'll see that it is not easy to talk to your parents about their ADLs and IADLs, but you will learn some door-opening techniques. You'll see that there are certain times when the subject begs to be discussed, and you'll be introduced to certain personal topics that you can talk about if you know how to be sensitive and tactful. This chapter also gives you a list of outside resources that can help you and your parents make day-to-day living just a little easier.

WHY TALK ABOUT THE ACTIVITIES OF DAILY LIVING

It's your parents' life; why should you tell them how to live it? There are lots of reasons to be involved in your elderly parents' day-to-day activities, but let's focus on these three:

- To avoid a crisis
- To give them permission to ask for help
- Because you love them

To Avoid a Crisis

Many conversations about the activities of daily living occur after a crisis. That's when Brian realized he should have talked to his father about showering without a no-slip mat or a grab bar. He got the call at work from the emergency room nurse who told him that his father had slipped in the shower and broken his hip.

Stephanie too knew she should have said something to her mom when she first noticed that her mom was losing weight. But it wasn't until the doctor called and said he was worried about her mother's problem with malnutrition that Stephanie thought about what she should say.

After the crisis, we're quick to rally around and put a no-slip mat in the tub and fill up the refrigerator with nutritious food. But the real benefit comes when we can talk about things like eating, bathing, and dressing before there is a problem.

To Give Them Permission to Ask for Help

It can be hard for elderly parents to admit they are having trouble managing the details of daily living. It is even harder to ask for help. Seventy-nine-year-old Marian had struggled with arthritis for years, and her children knew her hands were twisted and painful. But they had no idea that there were days when the arthritis made it impossible for Marian to take care of herself. She could not hold a toothbrush or button her blouse. She couldn't lift a pot off the stove or wash the dishes. She suffered in silence, however, because she was afraid that if anyone knew about her problems she would be put in a nursing home. Because she wouldn't talk to anyone about her physical difficulties, she had no idea that there were assistive devices and support services that could help her live on her own with greater comfort and ease.

If you talk to your parents and let them know that you realize how difficult it can be to keep up on day-to-day tasks like washing, cooking, and cleaning, they may not be as afraid to admit when they are having trouble. If you let them know that you want to help them live independently and comfortably, or if you stress to them that you want them to be able to remain in their home, they will become more willing to tell you when they need help.

Because You Love Them
Older adults know what busy lives their children lead; they may worry that if their children hear about their personal problems with day-to-day tasks they will become annoyed or even angry. Many seniors worry that they will become a burden and inconvenience others. But if you bring to the subject an attitude of concern rather than impatience and annoyance, you show you are aware of these problems and don't mind talking about them.

This message of love is delivered in the way you choose your words. There is quite a difference between the message in "Dad, you've got to wash your shirts more often; they really are starting to smell" and the one conveyed by "Dad, I'm doing a load of laundry later; why don't I stop by your house on my way home, pick up some of your shirts, and throw them in too?"

WHEN TO TALK ABOUT THE ACTIVITIES OF DAILY LIVING

Every contact you have with your parents creates a possible opportunity to talk about how well they are handling the activities of daily living. Keeping in regular touch (even if only by phone or e-mail) provides an open door to ask conversational questions like "What are you having for dinner tonight?" or "How's that old washing machine holding up?" or "Is your back still giving you trouble? Do you have any trouble bending over when you want to tie your shoes?" If you keep up an ongoing dialogue that shows concern and interest in the small things that make up your parent's day, you'll be more likely to know when he or she is in trouble.

In addition to your everyday conversations, you should also talk to your parent when you see a silent cue that causes you concern. You'll pick up these cues if you keep an eye open for potential problems when you visit your parent. If you see an empty refrigerator or one filled with old and moldy food, that's a cue to you that you need to talk about your parent's diet and overall health. (Some elderly who have lost sharp vision and sense of smell may not even know that the food in their cabinets is not fresh or that their clothes are not clean.) Do you see evidence of cooking problems, such as a burned pan or charred stove burners? Do you see your mom wearing clothes that are inappropriate for the weather? If you take your dad to the food store, does he buy $15 worth of food to last him for the month? All of these are silent cues that you shouldn't let pass without having a conversation that expresses your concern and offers your help.

Along with what you see at your parent's home, keep your ears open for masked cues your parent may send you. They're often easy to miss. If your mom says, "Can you stop by and have a cup of coffee with me?" it might be a sign that she is not eating regularly because she misses the social aspect of eating (which is a very important part of our food culture). If your dad says, "When your mother was alive, I never realized how hard it is to keep clothes clean," he might be asking for some help.

If you stay alert to the things you see and hear which indicate that your parents may be having a problem with the activities of daily living, you'll find many opportunities to talk about these sensitive subjects without appearing intrusive.

WHAT YOU SHOULD TALK ABOUT

Think about your own day. In the first hour or so, you probably get up, use the toilet, wash, dress, eat, and straighten up the house. These activities that you take for granted can be very difficult for the elderly to manage. In fact there is no end to the topics of self-care that you might talk about with your parents.

Breaking the Ice
When you first show interest in your parents' activities of daily living, they may balk at the intrusion—so go slowly. Talk about self-care in small bits of conversation—repeatedly. The first time Dot suggested to her mom that she should use a tub chair for bathing, for example, her mom quickly brushed off the idea as ridiculous. Dot let the subject drop, but the effort wasn't wasted. She had at least introduced the idea of a tub chair. A while later, Dot mentioned in casual conversation that someone she knew had just bought her dad a tub chair and explained how it helped him be more independent. A few weeks later, Dot brought her mom a catalogue that showed a picture of a tub chair and asked her to think about buying one. No pressure, no arguments, no dictates—just conversation and suggestions.

Over time, your comments and conversational tidbits about ways to make the activities of daily living easier to handle will help your parents at least think about taking actions that can preserve their independence for as long as possible.

Addressing Specific Issues

Whatever specific problem your parent may have with day-to-day activities, the primary message you want to convey is one that says, "I want to support you in your independence as best I can."

You might say: "I heard a person on TV talking about older persons who live in their own homes, and she said that there are lots of things seniors can do to make sure they can live independently longer. I thought some of the ideas were very good ones that you'd like to know about, because I know how important it is to you to be able to take care of yourself."

Then discuss whatever topic you want to talk about. Some subjects you might chat about include the following:

- Diet
- Making life easier
- Safety issues
- Opportunities for information

Talk About Diet.   A good nutritious diet is a vital part of healthy living, but for the elderly (especially those who live alone), three solid meals a day is often more than they can manage. Your parent may feel she can't afford to buy good food. Or she may not have the will or energy to prepare appetizing meals. She may skip meals simply because she is alone and doesn't feel like putting time or effort into something that's just for herself. Conversations with you about diet and nutrition will give your parent food for thought (so to speak).

If your own diet of bagels and coffee makes you hesitant to talk to your parent about his diet, look for news and magazine articles that focus on the nutritional needs of the elderly and use them as your expert source. Suggest that your parent discuss nutrition with a physician or dietician.

You might say: "I was just reading this article about how many senior citizens are undernourished because their daily diet lacks basic nutrients. This made me think about your diet. Do you have enough fresh fruits and vegetables in the house?"

When you know for certain that your parent is not eating properly, you should address the problem from a position of concern. *You might say:*

> "When I was growing up, you always made sure that I had good food and proper nutrition. Now that you're by yourself, I see that you aren't eating as well as you used to. I'm concerned about this. How can I help you with this?"
>
> "Let's look into arranging for food to be delivered to your house."
>
> "Would you like to come over to eat with us more often?"
>
> "Let's make some meals that we can separate into small portions and freeze so it's easy for you to prepare a good meal every day."

Talk About Making Life Easier.   As your parent ages, such everyday activities as bathing, dressing, and grooming can become difficult to do. If you notice that her appearance is looking a bit shabby occasionally, take that as a cue that she may be having some trouble with ordinary tasks like washing, buttoning, zippering, tying bows, and so on. Talk to her about gadgets that many people (not just the elderly) use to make life easier.

You might say: "Hey Mom, I came across this catalogue that has all kinds of household assistive devices that I've never seen before. Did you know that there are knob covers made of rubber so you can turn faucets and doorknobs easier? There are elastic shoelaces that let you slip on tie shoes without every having to tie the laces. There are watches with Velcro straps. Take a look at this catalogue; it has some great things in it."

You might say: "Dad, I bought myself a gadget that makes it easy to open twist-off tops from bottles and jars. I thought you might like one too."

You might say: "Look at this pill case I bought for you. I remembered when you weren't sure last week if you had taken your morning pills. I thought you'd like this. It has compartments for every day of the week so you can be sure you take the right pills at the right time. Let's sit down and put all your pills in here. I'm eager to see how it works."

Talk About Safety Issues. There are many aspects of daily living that can be dangerous for the elderly. If you notice that your parent has begun to burn food, is losing her hearing, is not able to read fine print (like the kind on medicine bottles), or seems unsteady on her feet, it's time to talk about ways to keep her safe and still independent.

You might say: "I've noticed that you're having a little trouble getting in and out of the car. I'll bet it's also hard to get in and out of your tub. I've been thinking that it would be a good idea to put down a no-slip bath mat and to install a grab bar."

You might say: "Here, I bought you this magnifying glass. It will help you read that tiny print on medicine bottles. I have one at home, and I use it all the time."

You might say: "I noticed when you stood up that you're having a little trouble staying steady on your feet. It's really going to slow you down if you fall and break a bone. You'd be more likely to stay healthy and independent if you used a cane or a walker. Let's talk to your doctor about that."

You might say: "I bought you this kitchen timer. I use one all the time when I put a pan or pot on the stove, and I want to remind myself that I have food cooking. I get involved in other things and forget, so this keeps me from burning dinner. Try it; it's really very helpful."

You might say: "If you really want to stay in your own home, then I'm going to help you make it safe. I'll be over on Saturday morning, and we'll put rug tape on the edges of your rugs, get night-lights in the halls, and fix the rickety banister."

Talk About Opportunities for Information.   Area hospitals, medical centers, senior centers, and other health-related facilities periodically present health fairs and workshops that provide valuable information free of charge. Keep your eyes open for these kinds of opportunities that will give both you and your parents information that will help them live independently and will open the door to further conversations about personal topics.

You might say: "I see that on Saturday the hospital is having a health fair for senior citizens. Are you going to go over and check it out? Would you like company?"

You might say: "Did you know that the American Association of Retired Persons has informational brochures that you can get for free? I thought I'd give them a call to see if they have something you'd like to read."

You might say: "I heard that the local senior center is having a free conference on diet and nutrition. That's something I think we could both use a lesson in. Will you go and bring me back whatever brochures and information they give out?"

If your parent doesn't want to call for information or attend workshops or conferences, you can certainly do the legwork and pick up handouts and information that you can use to bring up sensitive issues.

You might say: "I stopped by that health fair and picked up this pamphlet on safety-proofing a bathroom. I think I might make some of these changes in my own bathroom. There are a few things you might be interested in doing in your bathroom too. Here, take a look."

You might say: "Look what I got in the mail today. It's a listing of all the services available to senior citizens in your area. It tells you who to call if, for example, you want meals delivered to the house, or if you need a ride to the store, or if you need at-home medical attention. Keep this in a handy place. I think it's a great resource for you."

The challenge when talking to your parents about the activities of daily living is to make them understand that accepting help and finding ways to compensate for weakness is not a sign of frailty—it is a sign of spirit, independence, and determination.

RESOURCES

The American Association of Retired Persons (AARP) publishes a booklet called "Tools and Gadgets for Independent Living," which lists a variety of products that make life easier—and safer. To request a free copy (ask for document number 17035), write to:

AARP Fulfillment
601 E Street NW
Washington, DC 20049

The Mature Mart
P.O. Box 545
Jesup, GA 31545
(800) 720-6278 (voice)
(404) 881-9855 (fax)
www.maturemart.com (website)
orders@maturemart.com (e-mail)

This one-stop online shopping mall features more than twenty thousand products for daily living, personal care, dressing, and more. Products include a car door opener, easy-to-grip scissors and nail clippers, pill reminders, and a pedal exerciser.

Mail Order Medical Supply (MOMS)
24700 Rockefeller Avenue
Valencia, CA 91355
(800) 232-7443 (voice)
www.momsup.com

MOMS offers a home health care catalogue featuring products for daily living, such as ribbed doorknob covers, padded eating utensils, a walker cane with a built-in reacher, a folding shower bench, and other items for persons experiencing difficulties with ADLs or IADLs.

Center for Assistive Technology
515 Kimball Tower
University of Buffalo
Buffalo, NY 14214
(716) 829-3141 (voice)
(716) 829-3217 (fax)
wings.buffalo.edu

The Center for Assistive Technology conducts research and provides education and service to increase knowledge about assistive devices for persons with disabilities. The center operates Project LINK, a service that links consumers with assistive device companies related to their needs. The toll-free number for Project LINK is (800) 628-2281.

EXPERT HELP

This chapter was written with the expert help of Jane Hunley, MSSW, LMSW, a social worker who has been counseling geriatric patients and their families for fifteen years. She currently works at Parkland Memorial Hospital, Dallas, Texas.

Driving Safety

There are thirteen million people over the age of seventy on the road today. It's anticipated that there will be thirty million by the year 2020. If there are any complications related to age and driving, those complications will be exacerbated as we move forward into the twenty-first century.

Barbara L. Spreitzer-Berent, gerontologist
and founder of AgeQuest

Before her retirement, Tally was a high school principal—sharp, quick, and very intelligent. Now, well into her seventies, she's losing ground. "She's becoming forgetful, more so each day, it seems," her daughter says. "She drives, gets lost for hours, but eventually makes it back home. Last week she was in a car accident that has really made me start to worry about her ability to drive." Tally was not injured in the accident, but the telephone pole she crashed into could have been a car full of people. It could have been a pedestrian waiting to cross the street. It could have been a school bus, and it could have been a young child walking hand-in-hand with his mom. "She was upset by the accident, but now I don't think she even remembers it. Everyone in the family has tried to discourage her from driving, but we also see her point. Out here in the suburbs, she'd be stranded without a car. She couldn't go to visit her friends, see the doctor, or even get to the train station. I don't know the answer."

Because of a lack of awareness of the aging process or because of an independent (read that "stubborn") attitude, some older adults like Tally may not be as alert to their declining driving capabilities as they need to be. But research shows that the majority of older adults are capable of monitoring their own driving performance and making adjustments accordingly. So there is no magic age and no strict criteria that require an immediate revocation of a person's driving license due to the aging process. In fact, most experts agree that it's important to allow the elderly to drive as long as safely possible. Finding that line between safe and unsafe can be tricky, however. Driving safety and capability are touchy subjects that many of us may need to talk to our elderly parents about.

This chapter gives you guidelines regarding when to talk to your parents about their driving skills, what to say to them, and how to keep them off the road when it becomes absolutely necessary to do so.

WHY TALK ABOUT DRIVING SAFETY

Your parents know that strength, flexibility, good vision, hearing, and reaction times are all required to drive safely and that all may be affected by the aging process. No doubt they would agree with the studies which show that older drivers are more likely than younger ones to die or become seriously injured in a crash because their bodies are less able to withstand a crash impact. And they have also heard about the studies saying that older drivers are more likely than younger ones to be involved in multivehicle crashes (such as those at intersections) that often hurt others as well.

Despite these general statistics, it can be difficult for the elderly to realize when the deterioration of driving skills is affecting their *own* driving abilities. It often takes an outside observer—like you— to bring driving problems to their attention.

Clara's dad was very quick to point out older drivers who were a safety menace. He hated to get behind "old Sunday drivers" who couldn't see over the steering wheel and hogged the road. But Clara noticed that lately he himself was showing signs of deteriorating driving skills. When he drove her to a recent family party, she found herself gripping the seat with white knuckles as he ignored stop signs and occasionally bumped the curb. The ride home in the dark was worse; apparently he couldn't see street signs and twice missed their exit off the highway. "That night I knew he needed a reality check on his driving skills and an appointment with an eye doctor," remembers Clara. "There was no way he was going to admit this himself, but I knew somebody was going to get badly hurt if I didn't speak up."

Clara knew it was time to talk to her dad because she saw that his driving skills were declining and that safety was now an issue. According to the Insurance Institute for Highway Safety, there are a few more reasons why you should talk to an elderly parent about driving skills:

- Age-related declines in cognitive and sensory functions (for example, vision or hearing), and physical impairments due to medical conditions may affect some older people's driving ability.

- Motor-vehicle-related death rates per 100,000 for people seventy years old or older are higher than for people in any other group except those younger than twenty-five.
- Per mile driven, drivers seventy-five years old or older have higher rates of motor vehicle crashes that result in someone's death than do drivers in all other age groups except teenagers.
- Older people who are injured in motor vehicle crashes are more likely to die of their injuries than are people in other age groups.

WHEN TO TALK ABOUT DRIVING SAFETY

A dialogue about driving skills should begin early, when your parents are still independent drivers. You might begin by talking about news articles you read about accidents involving elderly drivers or proposed legislation to test elderly drivers. These topics invite your parents to talk about their feelings regarding driving and the elderly from an objective viewpoint. This kind of nonthreatening discussion establishes the topic of driving and the elderly as something you can talk about together without your immediately sounding accusatory. If over the years you keep this kind of dialogue going, you've laid the groundwork to make it easier to talk about your own parents' driving skills when you begin to have reason for concern.

An early dialogue about driving skills is also a good way to make sure your parents stay on the road as long as possible. If you put off talking until it's time to take away a person's license, you've missed many opportunities along the way to have postponed that drastic step.

The subject of driving skills and safety should definitely be put on the table when you notice any of the following red flags indicating there may be a problem with your parent's ability to drive safely:

- A pattern of close calls, violations, or collisions, even if they're minor
- Consistent and increasing difficulty in noticing pedestrians, signs, objects, or other vehicles; being surprised by passing cars; braking harder than normal for hazards, stop signs, or stopped traffic; going through red lights or stop signs; turning too fast or too slow; backing into or over objects; running over curbs
- Observable decline in physical abilities: difficulty in coordinating hand and foot movements; worsening discomfort from glare of oncoming headlights; difficulty in turning head, neck, and shoulders; slowed or erratic reactions; difficulty in keeping the car centered in a lane
- Observable change in emotions: undue nervousness behind the wheel; increased anger or frustration while driving; times of intense grief
- Rapid onset of fatigue from driving
- Observable decline in mental abilities: no longer using turn signals or mirrors; driving more slowly; becoming confused in simple driving situations; getting lost; making poor or slow decisions in traffic; hitting the accelerator instead of the brake, or vice versa
- Increasing number of confrontations with other drivers who honk their horns, tailgate, or pass aggressively
- Medical conditions that may impair driving, whether directly or as a result of medications: multiple sclerosis, Parkinson's, ALS, Alzheimer's disease, seizure disorders, sleep disorders, uncontrolled diabetes

Whenever you talk to your parent about her driving skills, avoid all-or-nothing actions, such as rushing to hide the keys at the first sign of a driving problem. Because driving gives us all a great degree of independence, older people need to hold on to that ability for as long as possible.

Mike wasn't ready to wait for his dad to have a major accident before he did something about his declining driving skills. Last Saturday night, Mike's dad drove him home from work while Mike's car was in for repair. "It was a nightmare," Mike told his wife the next day. "He rode right past the exit—I don't think he can see at night any more. I want him off the road. On Monday, I'm going to go over and take his keys. He's really going to hurt himself or someone else."

Although Mike's intentions are good, he is overreacting. It may be that his dad has trouble seeing at night and needs to have his eyes checked for cataracts. Many times there are certain adjustments that can be made to increase the safety factor without taking elderly people off the road. If poor night vision affects your parent's safety after dark, for example, talk about restricting driving to daytime hours. If he tires easily or gets disoriented in new places, then suggest he run errands close to home. If she's uncomfortable driving at high speeds, ask her to stay off the highway. If rush-hour traffic confuses and upsets her, encourage her to schedule her appointments at other times of the day. Don't overreact when you notice a driving problem; there are many steps between having a problem and being totally incapable.

WHAT YOU SHOULD TALK ABOUT

Conversations about driving safety should be ongoing and should cover the many stages of declining driving skills. It's best to break the ice with early discussions when you first notice a possible problem and then move on to addressing specific problems as they come up.

Breaking the Ice

At first, your conversations with your parent should focus on his own awareness of his driving skills and on finding ways to maintain his driving independence. You can do this in two steps:

1. Open the door to the subject.
2. Make an observation and then make a suggestion about how to handle the situation.

Open the Door to the Subject. Begin by making an observation and then stepping back and listening. This will give you an idea about how your mom or dad feels about driving and the aging process.

You might say: "My friend Bob wants to get his dad to stop driving at night because he has cataracts and can't see very well in the dark, but he doesn't want to get his dad upset. I guess that can be a really hard conversation to have."

Or, more specifically: "Dad, I see a few small dents and scratches on your car. What's been happening?"

Make an Observation and Then Make a Suggestion About How to Handle the Situation. You don't have to insist on anything. Just pose a possibility as food for thought. You might suggest a medical checkup so that a physician can evaluate the physical skills necessary for safe driving and offer ways to stay in peak physical form. (Even doing a few simple exercises in the morning can help your dad brake more quickly or look over his shoulder more easily before changing lanes.)

You might say: "Mom, I've noticed that you're having trouble seeing traffic signs. Maybe it's time to see your eye doctor and check on your prescription, and I think it might help to sit on a pillow so you can see the road better."

To keep your parent on the road as long as possible, you might also suggest that he

- Avoid nighttime driving
- Drive only to familiar locations
- Avoid highways and rush-hour traffic
- Avoid driving alone

Addressing Specific Issues

When you see signs that your parent is losing the skills needed to drive safely, you'll need to address specific issues. What you will say to your parent about her driving habits depends on her level of mental competence or incompetence. The following five steps (adapted from Barbara L. Spreitzer-Berent's publication, "Supporting the Mature Driver") follow a person's progressive deterioration of skills:

1. Offer specific ways to improve driving skills.
2. Encourage action by drawing on your personal relationship.
3. Take action.
4. Explore alternative transportation options.
5. Take the keys.

Offer Specific Ways to Improve Driving Skills.   You can contact AARP (see the Resources section at the end of this chapter) or the occupational therapy department of your local hospital to find a driver evaluation center. Here professionals evaluate a driver's physical and mental performance with written, visual, and performance tests; provide on-the-road training; help the driver acquire and use adaptive equipment to compensate for physical limitations; and suggest specific physical and mental exercises that the driver can use to improve his driving skills. Also look for driver's refresher courses through senior citizen centers, hospitals, retirement communities, or civic organizations.

You might say: "I heard that AARP offers driver's education courses for senior citizens. A lot of older people who take these classes find they can safely stay on the road much longer than those who don't. How about I get a schedule of those classes and sign you up? I'll even go with you if you like."

Encourage Action by Drawing on Your Personal Relationship.
Discussing driving skill with your parent requires great diplomacy. If she feels that your words are accusing, criticizing, threatening, or embarrassing, she's less apt to listen and more likely to argue with you. Talk with concern and love.

You might say: "The number of near misses you've had on the road lately is a real concern to me. I'm worried that you're going to be in an accident and hurt yourself or somebody else. For me, could you please go for a driving evaluation?"

Take Action.
When you're sure your parent is risking his safety when he's behind the wheel, it's time to do something about it.

You might say: "I absolutely am not comfortable with you driving down to your winter vacation home this year, so I've bought you a plane ticket and made arrangements for your car to be driven down for you."

Explore Alternative Transportation Options.
Before taking away the keys for good, help your parent get used to other kinds of travel.

You might suggest that you take the wheel more often. Take the bus with your dad the next time the two of you visit the doctor's office. Find out the names and phone numbers of local agencies that will take him to church or the grocery store. Buy him a gift certificate from a local taxi or limousine company that he can use when he needs to travel.

You might say: "I was thinking that someday it might happen that you can't use your car to get to your doctor appointment—maybe there will be snow on the road, maybe you won't be feeling so good, maybe your vision will be weak. So I think it would be a good idea to find out how you can get there without your car. When you go to the doctor's next Tuesday, I'll come with you and we'll go on the bus. It's good to know how to use public transportation once in a while."

Take the Keys.   If a medical professional has said that your parent can no longer drive at all under any circumstance, your conversation will need to be short and direct and your actions much more specific.

You might say: "The doctor has said that you can no longer drive. I'm sorry, but for your safety and the safety of others, we'll need to find other ways to get you to all the places you want to go."

Don't forget that driving cessation is a life-altering event. You can't lay down the law, take the keys, and expect your parent to agree and that's that. More likely, you will find that (as with most major life changes) your parent will need to go through the steps of denial, resistance, and exploration before she can accept the new order of things. When you talk to your parent about driving safety, anticipate an emotional reaction and some resistance.

When you have no choice but to take away the car keys, your parent will be more willing to accept the idea if you can reduce the emotional impact of this decision. Perhaps your dad would feel better keeping the car "just for emergencies" (while you hide the keys). Maybe your mom wouldn't mind letting you drive her to her appointments if the two of you can stop for a bite to eat afterwards.

BEYOND TALKING

After several car accidents and innumerable close calls, Ken asked his eighty-four-year-old father to give up his car keys. His father said no. Ken tried being understanding but firm; he tried being demanding; he tried reasoning; he tried appealing to his dad's sense of responsibility to others on the road. Nothing worked. Finally, when his dad began to talk about a two-day car trip to visit his brother, Ken knew that the time for talking was over. It was time to take action.

If talking to your parent about giving up the keys is not working, you might have to take other actions to keep her off the road. Install a car alarm that will alert you or someone nearby if the car door is opened, install a security lock that is too complicated for your parent to open, ask a mechanic to show you how to disable the car, or simply sell the car.

Remember that police departments have the authority to request that the Department of Motor Vehicles (DMV) order a motorist to undergo a driver reexamination, medical evaluation, or both. Usually it's the police who take the initiative and make this request to the DMV after an incident involving an older driver whose judgment and perception seem to be failing. But police departments also can file the request on behalf of worried family members. You can make the request for reexamination yourself by contacting your state DMV and asking for the appropriate form. Anonymous requests, however, are not accepted.

A person who is notified by the DMV that a driver reexamination or medical evaluation is required can challenge the request at a DMV administrative hearing, but she can't ignore it. To do so is to have her driver's license automatically suspended.

Whatever conversations you have about driving cessation, it's very important to remain patient and open to ideas that help your parent save face and preserve his dignity. The subject of driving safety is much more emotional than you might think—approach it with care and empathy. If you must take the keys, make sure you allow your parent to vent his anger and express all the emotional pain that comes with losing driving independence.

RESOURCES

The Association for Driver Rehabilitation
P.O. Box 49
Edgerton, WI 53534
(608) 884-8833

A representative of this organization can give you the location of a driver evaluation and rehabilitation center near you.

AARP publishes a booklet called "The Older Driver Skill Assessment and Resource Guide: Creating Mobility Choices." To request a free copy (ask for document no. D14957), write to:

AARP Fulfillment
601 E Street NW
Washington, DC 20049

AARP also offers a driver's refresher course called the 55 Alive Mature Driver Program. For information, call toll free: (888) 227-7669.

The American Automobile Association (AAA) publishes a booklet called "Drivers 55 Plus: Test Your Own Performance" (publication no. 362). To purchase a single copy, send a check for $2 to:
AAA Foundation for Traffic Safety
P.O. Box 8257
Fredericksburg, VA 22404
(800) 305-SAFE

AAA also offers a driver's course called Safe Driving for Mature Operators. Call a local AAA branch listed in the phone book for information.

The National Safety Council offers a driver's course called Coaching the Mature Driver. For information, call (800) 621-6244.

EXPERT HELP

This chapter was written with the expert help of Barbara L. Spreitzer-Berent, a gerontologist and the founder of AgeQuest, a training and consulting company dedicated to addressing topics of interest to older and midlife adults, family caregivers, and professionals in the field of aging. She has conducted hundreds of training seminars for professional and family caregivers. She is also an older-driver educator for AARP and AAA. Spreitzer-Berent serves as a consultant on numerous projects related to senior transportation and participates as an adjunct faculty member in the gerontology department at Madonna University in Livania, Michigan. Her newest publication, "Supporting the Mature Driver: A Handbook for Friends, Family Members and Advisors," is currently available by contacting: Quest Learning Resources L.L.C., P.O. Box 1481, Royal Oak, MI 48068; (248) 547-4618.

Late-Onset Alcoholism

Alcoholism is harder to detect in the elderly than in any other population, but once the problem is identified, outcome studies show that they have the highest rate of recovery.

*Carol Colleran, director of older adult services
for Hanley-Hazelden Center*

Trish was worried about her mom, Diana. During her recent weekend visit she noticed signs of aging that she hadn't seen before. Diana's hands were shaking as she tried to pour her morning coffee. Later in the day she seemed unsteady on her feet. "Maybe she's going to need a cane or a walker," Trish thought. Diana's speech also seemed slurred, and Trish wondered if her dentures no longer fit properly. All these questions were abruptly answered the moment Trish opened her mother's bedroom door to say goodnight and found her passed out on the bed with an empty bottle of scotch lying at her side. Suddenly all the pieces fit. Trish's mom wasn't showing signs of aging; she was showing signs of an alcohol problem.

L ate-onset alcoholism can be very difficult to detect in the elderly and especially difficult to talk about. Some of the common symptoms of alcoholism—shaking hands, forgetfulness, napping, falling accidents—are also typical signs of the aging process, so the problem frequently goes undetected. There is also a hesitation to talk to the elderly about a drinking problem because people often think, "What harm is he doing?" or "At her age, what difference does it make?"

This chapter answers these questions and gives you the words you need to talk to your parent if you suspect he or she may have an alcohol problem.

WHY TALK ABOUT LATE-ONSET ALCOHOLISM

You should talk to your parent if you suspect he has an alcohol problem for the same reasons you would talk to anyone you love about a habit that can kill him. That's not saying he will want to listen or that he will welcome your advice right away. But it does mean that because elderly alcoholics are at such high risk of illness and injury, someone who loves them and has their best interests at heart needs to step in and make an effort to help. Who better than you?

In addition to showing love and concern, you should talk to your parent about her drinking problem because, as this section explains:

- Quitting can improve both physical and emotional health
- Old age makes the problem even worse
- Mixing alcohol and medication can be deadly

- Chances of recovery are high
- Your parent will listen to you

**Because Quitting Can Improve
Both Physical and Emotional Health**

Experts agree that stopping an alcohol problem in the elderly improves the quality of life for people who may very well live another five, ten, or even twenty-five years. Failing to do something about the problem not only will negatively affect the person's quality of life but also can worsen diseases normally associated with aging, such as heart and liver disease, arthritis, diabetes, glaucoma, cataracts, hearing loss, pancreatitis, colitis, ulcers, gastritis, and Alzheimer's disease.

When Jim's father began to spend most of his days in a drunken stupor, Jim was annoyed because it was embarrassing to have the neighbors hear him singing at the top of his lungs and see him staggering around the backyard. But he figured it wasn't his place to judge his father, who he knew was very lonely since Jim's mom died. "I figured that he wasn't hurting anyone," said Jim, "and it probably helped him ease the pain of being retired and widowed. But now I wish I could go back and do something to help him stop drinking. I wasn't thinking about how hard it would be to live the rest of his life like that, and I never thought it would kill him." But it did. Jim's dad lost his balance one afternoon and hit his head on the edge of a table as he fell forward. He suffered a severe brain trauma and lapsed into a coma before Jim found him several hours later. Two days later, Jim's dad died. A conversation about his drinking problem may have saved his life, but Jim was afraid it wasn't his business.

Talking to your parent about a drinking problem is in many circumstances a matter of life and death. It's not something you should put off any longer.

Because Old Age Makes the Problem Even Worse

You should talk to your parent about alcohol abuse because this problem is especially dangerous for older people. As the metabolism slows down with age, it takes longer to eliminate alcohol from the bloodstream. Because the body changes the way it metabolizes alcohol, a person can develop a drinking problem late in life without even increasing her daily intake of alcohol. Drinking two or three beers at age sixty-five is like drinking ten or twelve beers at age twenty. It's a good bet that your parent doesn't know this.

No one was more surprised than Kip's dad when the doctor told him he had an alcohol problem. He had been having two martinis before dinner and another two before bedtime for the last forty years. How could he have a drinking problem all of a sudden? This change in metabolism was the reason, but because no one had warned Kip's dad, he was caught up in an addiction before he knew what had happened.

If you see signs that your parent's usual drinking pattern is now causing her trouble, this is a good reason to sit down for a talk.

Because Mixing Alcohol and Medication Can Be Deadly

The effects of alcohol are intensified by many of the prescription medications commonly taken by the elderly. And the action of some drugs (such as anticonvulsants, anticoagulants, and antidiabetes drugs) is exaggerated when combined with alcohol, causing unexpected health problems. It is also very dangerous (and can even be fatal) to mix alcohol with such drugs as tranquilizers, sleeping pills, painkillers, and antihistamines. Your parent may have no idea that his lifelong social drinking habits and his doctor-prescribed or "safe" over-the-counter drugs can cause serious problems.

Rachel's mom was always a moderate social drinker who never once appeared drunk in public. Never—until about six months ago.

The ladies in her church group were appalled when she staggered into their spring meeting, and she caused quite a stir when she had to be carried out of her granddaughter's wedding reception after she became "falling-down drunk." Her children could not believe that their mother would ever, ever drink too much. But there she was, out cold on the floor. Rachel took her mom to the doctor the next morning and explained what had been going on. After looking over her medical chart, the doctor knew exactly why the alcohol was having such a powerful effect. One of her new medications was known to intensify the effect of alcohol. Every single glass of wine Rachel's mom drank caused her body to react as if it were five glasses. Over time, her body had become sensitized to alcohol, and now she was showing the results.

If your parents drink alcohol and take prescription or over-the-counter medications, you need to talk to them and to their physician about how each one reacts with the other.

Because Chances of Recovery Are High

Another reason to talk to your parent about a suspected alcohol problem is that seniors (especially those with late-onset alcoholism) have the highest recovery rate of all age groups. On the whole, this group is most willing to accept the authority of a health care practitioner who says they must change their drinking or medication pattern. They are also most anxious about maintaining their mental faculties and avoiding nursing homes.

Because Your Parent Will Listen to You

Experts say that the family has the most influence on older adults. Your wishes and concerns are very important to your parent—you, over anyone else, may be the only person who can convince him to get help for an alcohol problem.

WHEN TO TALK ABOUT
LATE-ONSET ALCOHOLISM

Before going to bed, Hank called his dad to remind him that he would be stopping by in the morning to borrow his ladder. As soon as his dad gave a slurred "Hello," Hank knew he was drinking heavily again. "That's it," Hank thought. "I'm going over there right now and having a talk with him. We've got to find some way to get him off that booze before he kills himself!"

Hank is right about needing to talk to his dad, but this is not the time. When you do decide that you should talk to your parent about her drinking or medication habits, choose a time when she is most likely to be alert and receptive. Never bring up the subject when she is obviously under the influence; this is not the time for a calm, constructive conversation. When picking the best time, keep in mind that most alcoholics are never completely sober at the end of the day; instead, this is the time when they will be most argumentative and defensive. So choose the time for your discussion carefully. You should choose a good time to talk when you notice these situations:

- When your parent is having trouble dealing with life changes
- When your parent's social life revolves around almost-daily cocktail parties
- When your parent is involved in the care of your children
- When your parent needs medical attention for other physical or mental problems
- When you notice warning signs of alcoholism

When Your Parent Is Having Trouble
Dealing with Life Changes

Carl's dad retired from his job as plant supervisor at an electrical sub-station two weeks after his wife died. Carl remembers, "It was the worst thing that could have happened to my dad after my mother's death, but the retirement had been planned for months, and there was no turning back. Dad cancelled the reservations he had made for a weeklong retirement celebration at their favorite golf resort and sat home and drank all day. I didn't know how to console him or keep him busy. He just wanted to numb the pain."

Carl's dad is not a good-for-nothing drunk; he's a man in emotional pain. Late-onset alcoholics often begin abusing alcohol in response to life changes. They may turn to alcohol as a coping mechanism to deal with such life changes as lowered income, declining health, and the deaths of friends and relatives. Recently retired or widowed men are especially vulnerable. If your parent is having trouble dealing with life changes, be aware that his slurred speech and trembling hands may be more than a sign of aging; begin right away having conversations about the problem of alcohol abuse and the elderly.

When Your Parent's Social Life Revolves
Around Almost-Daily Cocktail Parties

Karen was happy to see that her parents had adjusted well to their move into a retirement community for active adults. Their social life was so hectic they scarcely had time to talk to her on the phone when she would call on the weekends. But Karen's delight quickly turned to concern when she paid a visit. "From the time I arrived on Friday night until I left on Sunday night, my parents sat around with their new friends drinking. They would gather for morning

Bloody Marys, move to the clubhouse for a liquid lunch, and then meet for a cocktail hour that never ended. I have never seen them drink that much in their entire lives—I'm really worried they both are heading for trouble."

Well-adjusted elders who are now retired with an active social life or who have moved to a retirement community are frequently at risk for excessive alcohol consumption if their social life revolves around almost-daily cocktail parties. If your parents talk a lot about these kinds of gatherings, you should begin an early dialogue about the problems associated with drinking and the elderly.

When Your Parent Is Involved in the Care of Your Children

"For very selfish reasons I didn't want to believe that my mother-in-law was drinking during the day when she was watching my four-year-old," says Marsha. "If it wasn't for her help, I never would have been able to go back to work. Every day she took my son to preschool, picked him up when it was over, and kept him at her house until I finished work. Her help was such a blessing. But I started thinking something was wrong when my son would talk about Grandma sleeping in the afternoon or driving 'wild' or talking 'funny.' One day his school called me at work because his grandmother had not picked him up. Worried she was sick or had fallen, I raced to her house and found her out cold in a drunken stupor. She was embarrassed and heartbroken, but I just couldn't leave my son with her anymore."

You should talk to your parent about your concerns if she is involved in the care of your children. Fear of losing time with grandchildren can motivate even the most obstinate older adult to take a serious look at unhealthy drinking habits. If you do not feel comfortable leaving your child alone with your parent, that's a good time to talk to her about this problem.

When Your Parent Needs Medical Attention
for Other Physical or Mental Problems

When your parent needs medical attention for other physical or mental problems, you have an open door to bring up the subject of alcohol abuse. Most late-onset alcoholics are identified when they seek treatment for something else; in fact, the House of Representatives Committee on Aging found that an estimated 70 percent of the admissions of the elderly to hospitals were for alcohol-related illness or injuries. This is why any medical problem that requires professional attention is a golden opportunity to ask a doctor to conduct an alcohol screening on your parent and to talk about the problems of late-onset alcoholism. In addition, you must talk to your parent and his doctor about a suspected or obvious alcohol problem before he has any kind of surgery. A delirium tremor is a complication that can occur in alcoholics who are suddenly deprived of alcohol during the postoperative period. The physician must be forewarned.

When You Notice Warning Signs of Alcoholism

You should talk to your parent about a possible problem with alcohol if he or she exhibits some of the following warning signs of trouble:

- Prefers attending a lot of events where drinking is accepted, such as luncheons, "happy hours," and parties
- Drinks in a solitary, hidden way
- Makes a ritual of having drinks before, with, or after dinner, and becomes annoyed when this ritual is disturbed

- Loses interest in activities and hobbies that used to bring pleasure
- Drinks in spite of warning labels on prescription drugs
- Is often intoxicated or slightly tipsy, and sometimes has slurred speech
- Disposes of large volumes of empty beer and liquor bottles and seems secretive about it
- Often has the smell of liquor on his or her breath or of mouthwash to disguise it
- Is neglecting personal appearance and gaining or losing weight
- Complains of constant sleeplessness, loss of appetite, or chronic health complaints that seem to have no physical cause
- Has unexplained burns or bruises and tries to hide them
- Seems more depressed or hostile than usual
- Can't handle routine chores and paperwork without making mistakes
- Has irrational or undefined fears or delusions, or seems under unusual stress
- Seems to be losing his or her memory

Many of these symptoms are often attributed to other diseases or are accepted as part of the aging process. However, many older people find that once they stop drinking these symptoms disappear.

WHAT YOU SHOULD TALK ABOUT

The experts who work with alcoholics can tell you without hesitation that arguing over alcohol abuse is not effective. No matter how much you debate, explain, or yell (or how often you pour alcohol down the drain), you will not change your parent's drinking habits.

The goal is to firmly state your feelings without getting emotional or judgmental so that you give your parent information to think about.

When you talk to your parent about this sensitive issue, you may have better results if you are respectful and speak in "I" statements rather than make finger-pointing judgmental statements. Instead of saying "You were drunk at Mary's party," you might say, "I felt very embarrassed when you drank too much at Mary's party." This simple shift of pronouns will reduce the resistance you get to this subject.

Breaking the Ice

To talk effectively about a subject as emotionally charged as alcohol and drugs, you need to be keenly aware of your parent's value system. She is likely to be especially sensitive to words like *alcoholism*, *drug abuse*, and *addiction* and will immediately reject your advice if you use these words. Instead, use the expression *a problem with alcohol* or *a problem with medications*. This semantic difference will influence the way she will respond.

Addressing Specific Issues

When talking about alcohol or drug problems, try to make your parent see that there are good reasons to get help for this problem. In your discussions, you might include the topics covered in this section:

- Why older persons drink to excess
- How alcohol can affect general health
- How alcohol can cause symptoms of senility
- How alcohol can cause injuries
- How your parent's drinking problem affects you and the family

- The common nature of the problem
- Excuses

Talk About Why Older Persons Drink to Excess.   Talk about why older persons may drink, rather than the disease itself. If you can see that your parent lacks coping skills to deal with the many changes in his life, is feeling isolated, lacks purpose, or is looking for more communication with an extended family, these are things you can talk about that can have a very direct influence on your parent's alcohol abuse.

You might say: "Dad, I can see that you haven't been very happy since you retired. I guess it's been very hard for you to adjust. Have you thought about ways you could use all your skills and experience that would keep you involved and happy?"

You might say: "Mom, it must be very hard for you to feel happy after so many of your good friends have died. How do you cope with that feeling?" (See also the chapter on grief and bereavement.)

You might say: "I miss your company. How about we make a date to talk on the phone every day and meet for dinner at least once a week?"

You might say: "Mom, I know we don't keep in touch as much as we would like, and I don't send you pictures of the kids like I promise, but I have thought of a way to improve. I'm going to teach you how to use the computer so I can easily send you e-mail and pictures. It'll be easy for me to do that every week, and it'll be easy for you to receive them."

It is important to understand that once they become alcoholic, they are no longer drinking for these reasons. They are now drinking because of the disease of alcoholism.

Talk About How Alcohol Can Affect General Health. Excessive drinking and misuse of medications can make it difficult for the elderly to stay healthy.

You might say: "I'm worried that your drinking will affect your overall health. Did you know that when you're drinking, some medical problems are hard to diagnose? Alcohol causes changes in your heart and blood vessels, for example, that can dull pain that might be a warning sign of a heart attack. And over time, heavy drinking permanently damages the brain and central nervous system, as well as the liver, heart, kidneys, and stomach. I'm afraid that if you keep drinking, you'll face major health problems in the future."

Talk About How Alcohol Can Cause Symptoms of Senility. Many older adults are very sensitive about being perceived as "senile" or are afraid of having Alzheimer's disease.

You might say: "I was reading an article the other day that said that excessive use of alcohol can cause symptoms similar to those of Alzheimer's disease, like forgetfulness, reduced attention, and confusion. It can also accelerate normal aging or cause premature aging of the brain. If incorrectly identified, such symptoms actually lead to unnecessary institutionalization. I'd really like you to talk to your doctor about your drinking so that your condition is not misdiagnosed as dementia. Maybe he can help you with this problem."

Talk About How Alcohol Can Cause Injuries. The elderly are very much aware that a bad fall or injury can put them out of action for a long time. They may not know that an estimated 70 percent of all hospitalized senior citizens and fully half of all nursing home residents have problems with alcohol.

You might say: "If you want to be independent and care for yourself in your own home, you need to stay away from alcohol. It's known to slow down brain activity, which impairs mental alertness, judgment, physical coordination, and reaction time. That's why it increases the risk of falls and accidents and causes many elderly people to end up in the hospital or a nursing home."

Talk About How Your Parent's Drinking Problem Affects You and the Family.   Your parent probably assumes that his drinking is not your business because it does not affect you. Tell him that it does. *You might say:*

> "I feel very worried about your health."
> "I feel embarrassed when I visit you and you've had too much to drink."
> "I'm afraid to leave my children in your care."

Talk About the Commonness of the Problem.   Because most seniors drink in their homes rather than in bars, and most do not drive while drunk, they don't see or hear about other elderly people who have a drinking problem. Talk about other seniors, family members, or the neighbor down the street who also has a problem like this. Talk about how these people are affected and what they're doing about it. In a comfortable way, use familiar names as examples.

You might say: "You are not the first person in our family to have this problem. Remember Uncle Felix? He refused to get help and ended up breaking a few bones when he fell down the stairs. He never really recovered physically from that fall. I don't want that to happen to you."

Talk About Excuses. When you talk to your parent about her drinking problem, she will probably have a ready supply of excuses. You should think about what you'll say to counter the excuse.

She may say that the problem is just a phase because she's feeling sad over a particular life event.
You might say: "You have to remember that alcohol [and sedatives] are depressants that will only make things worse."

He may say that his doctor knows how much alcohol or medication he takes and that the doctor says it's OK.
You might say: "I'm relieved to hear that you've discussed this with your doctor. But I'm afraid that he might not know how it's affecting you and exactly how much you're taking. I'd like to talk to him myself just to make sure you're not in any danger of overdoing it."

She may say that that she needs the tranquilizers to stay calm.
You might say: "There are many better ways to deal with stress—ways that are good for your body. Taking a daily walk will help. Going out with a friend when you feel stressed is a great tension reliever. In fact, I often do some very simple relaxation exercises like deep breathing and guided imagery that we can do together. They keep me calm, and they don't make me feel tired or drugged. I'll teach them to you."

He may say it makes no difference since he doesn't do anything all day anyway.
You might say: "You're right about not having much to do. I'll help you find some exciting ways to use your time. You might like volunteer work or activities at the senior citizen center or an educational course. Let's look into these things."

GETTING HELP

Pointing out the problem of alcohol abuse is the first step in helping your parent. Next you need to point him in the right direction for help. Alcoholism is not something that he alone can manage successfully. He needs professional help but will need your guidance to find it.

It's important to find a program that caters to older adults. They need more one-on-one care than younger people. Their support groups need to address the issues of the elderly: many older adults do not feel free to talk about their losses with younger people; they don't relate to young alcoholics; and their life transition issues are very different from those of other age groups. These differences can influence the success of their treatment.

In-patient treatment programs are best for this population for many reasons. Older adults generally need more medical attention. The treatment often takes longer. Some need specialized care for their reduced cognitive abilities. And the need to drive back and forth (often at night) to outpatient programs is often difficult for older adults and reduces their willingness to follow through.

Alcoholic treatment programs specifically for older adults are beginning to form throughout the country but are still sometimes difficult to find. Notable models are the Hanley-Hazelden Center in West Palm Beach, Florida; Chelsea Hospital in Ann Arbor, Michigan; and Wake Forest Hospital in Winston-Salem, North Carolina.

If your parent cannot travel to these types of facilities, then you need to take advantage of what's available locally. You can receive referrals from your parent's doctor, from local hospitals, from your clergy, or from Alcoholics Anonymous. Then you need to do thorough research. Call recommended facilities and find out what they offer the older adult that is distinct from a program for the general public. Assess the needs of your parent beyond the alcohol addiction and ask if the facility can accommodate these needs; for example, does the facility accommodate her need for a wheelchair or her hearing or vision difficulties? Does it accept Medicare payments? Does it have outpatient day programs so your parent doesn't have to drive at night? Does it offer transportation if your parent doesn't drive? You want to eliminate any obstacles that can interfere with the success of your parent's treatment experience.

In addition to a supervised medical program, hook your parent up with an older adult support group. Many of the Alcoholics Anonymous chapters are forming groups specifically for this older population.

You might say: "You are not alone. There are many senior citizens who have a problem with drinking. Many who have decided to stop drinking are happy to help other older people with this problem. Let's look into finding a support group that is made up of people your age."

Talking about late-onset alcoholism could vastly improve the quality of your parent's life—in fact, it may very well save his or her life.

RESOURCES

Alcoholics Anonymous, a national organization with chapters in all fifty states, provides meeting places where recovering alcoholics share their experiences with those who are still struggling with the disease. This free program is listed in the telephone directory under

Alcoholics Anonymous. Al-Anon Family Group is a branch of AA that is designed to help the family and friends of alcoholics; some branches offer a program called Adult Children of Alcoholics. Call (800) 433-2666 for information and referrals. In most urban areas, a central AA office, or Intergroup, staffed mainly by volunteer AA members, will be happy to answer your questions or put you in touch with those who can. Or you can write to:

AA World Services, Inc.
P.O. Box 459
New York, NY 10163
(212) 870-3400

Love First: A New Approach for Alcoholism and Drug Addiction
Jeff Jay and Debra Jay
Hazelden Guidebook, 2000
For a list of Hazelden books on older adults and addiction, see the Hazelden Transitions website at www.htbookplace.org.

National Clearinghouse for Alcohol and Drug Information
P.O. Box 2345
Rockville, MD 20852
(301) 468-2600
www.health.org

The National Institute on Alcohol Abuse and Alcoholism (NIAAA) provides information on alcohol abuse and alcoholism. Contact:

NIAAA
6000 Executive Boulevard
Bethesda, MD 20892-7003
(301) 443-3860

The National Council on Alcoholism and Drug Dependence, Inc., can refer you to treatment services in your area. Contact:
NCADD national headquarters
12 West Twenty-First Street, 8th floor
New York, NY 10010
(800) NCA-CALL (622-2255)

The National Institute on Aging (NIA) offers a variety of resources on health and aging. Contact:
NIA Information Center
P.O. Box 8057
Gaithersburg, MD 20898
(800) 222-2225
(800) 222-4225 (TTY)

EXPERT HELP

This chapter was written with the expert help of Carol Colleran, director of older adult services for Hanley-Hazelden Center in West Palm Beach, Florida, one of the first recovery centers in the country to develop a treatment program designed especially for older adults. Along with Debra Jay, Carol Colleran has written a Hazelden Guidebook on older adults and addiction, which will be published in January 2002.

Late-Life Romance

You may dig your heels in when your parent comes home with a new date. But on second thought, remember that your parents will be with you for only a short time, and if this makes those years happy, God bless them.

Paul A. Falzone, president and CEO of The Right One

Jed knew something was going on with his seventy-five-year-old mother. "I'm not the most observant guy," confesses Jed, "but I couldn't miss the new hairstyle, the touch of makeup, and the ear-to-ear grin she was wearing the last time we visited. I told her she was looking especially nice, and she blushed! 'Is there something you want to tell me?' I asked her. She hesitated for just a moment and then said 'No,' but I've got a gut feeling that she must have a new boyfriend. I guess it's none of my business, and if she doesn't want to tell me, that's her decision. I just hope she knows what she's doing."

Jed's instinct is right—his mom has a boyfriend—but his reaction is misguided. It's none of his business only if his mom says so, but

Jed never even asked. It's probably hard for his mom to "confess" to having romantic feelings and needs, and maybe she's just waiting for the right moment to share this new part of her life. Jed can open that door and offer assurances that he is happy about whatever makes her happy (even if he is unsure exactly how he feels), enabling her to talk to him without embarrassment.

How you talk to your parent about a new romance will of course depend in large part on how you feel about the subject, but in most cases, the experts agree that the rights of the elderly in the romantic arena should not be dictated by the feelings of their children. If your parent is in sound mental health, he or she does not need your permission or approval to have a love life, but certainly may like to talk to you about this important part of life. This chapter gives you an explanation of why you should want to talk to your parent about his or her romantic interests, when to talk about this subject, and what exactly you can say.

WHY TALK ABOUT A NEW ROMANCE

"I think he's out of his mind," Ted told his wife. "My father has been a widow for twenty-five years, and now that he's eighty years old he decides he needs a new wife? This is just crazy. Is he going to leave his estate to her when he dies? And is she then going to leave it to her kids? I know this sounds selfish, but it just doesn't seem right to me."

Ted's dad had been dating his fiancée for over five years, but they had not talked much about the relationship to their children for fear of what they might say. They worried that the "kids" might see this relationship as an act of disloyalty to their deceased spouses.

They thought that maybe there would be hard feelings and family arguments. They found it easier just to downplay their relationship publicly and enjoy in private the love and companionship they gave to each other. But now that they've decided to marry, this surprise news will surely cause hurt feelings and family disagreements.

The shock and anger that Ted is feeling is natural when an elderly parent suddenly decides to get married. But this situation isn't really sudden. If Ted had been willing to talk to his dad more openly about his dad's relationship with his girlfriend over the last five years, he would not be feeling so surprised now. Ted knew his dad was seeing a "lady friend." He knew they spent a lot of time together, but he never asked any questions. Both Ted and his dad felt uncomfortable with the situation, so they took the easy road of silence.

This situation points to a few of the many reasons you should talk to your parent about his love life. For starters it's an important part of his life, so of course you should encourage him to talk about it. If you want to have a close relationship with your parent, you should want him to feel comfortable talking to you about his feelings and hopes and disappointments. You don't need to know the personal details, but it's nice for your parent to know that you're interested and that you care.

You should also talk openly about your parent's friends so that she feels it is a "safe" subject. Like Ted's dad, she may not be sharing the details because she's afraid of how you'll react. To imagine how she feels, consider how you felt when you had a new girlfriend or boyfriend of whom you thought your parents might not approve. You probably kept quiet so you wouldn't have to hear your friend ridiculed or attacked. The tables are turned now, but the feelings are the same. You can't expect your parent to share this part of her life with you if she knows you'll have nothing nice to say.

It's also important to encourage your parent to talk to you about his romances if you are concerned for his well-being and safety. Remember when your parents wanted to know whom you were dating, where you were going, when you'd be back? Remember that they were concerned about the morals and upbringing of your dates? Now you know why. Because you know that there are many people who are quick to take advantage of the loneliness of senior citizens, it's natural to want to know if the person is someone of substance ethically and morally. This is not to say that your parent can't make a sound decision for himself, but your objective view might be more reliable. When someone you love becomes involved with another person, it's very natural for you to be concerned about the loved one's safety, security, and happiness.

WHEN TO TALK ABOUT A NEW ROMANCE

Open, honest communication is the best way to make sure a new romance doesn't turn into a disaster for your parent. But talking about your parent's love life isn't necessarily a "Sit down, let's have a talk" subject. Her social activities are a part of life that you can easily talk about in the same way you talk about the weather. If you talk to your parent casually and conversationally about her daily activities on a regular basis, the fact that she is going out to dinner with a special friend will naturally be discussed. This approach will give you the facts throughout the developing relationship, thus preventing your having to address the subject when the situation has grown serious and your parent is ready to make major life decisions.

Whether your parent's calendar is a social whirl of activity or he is a stay-at-home type, you should always be asking such questions as, "So, what have you been doing this week?" "Have you gone out with anyone interesting lately?" "Do you have any plans for the weekend?"

Listen for Hints
Your parent may begin to drop hints about a new friend to see how you'll react, before offering more information. She might say, "I saw Harry Smith yesterday at the supermarket. I always thought Harry was such a nice person." You can absentmindedly say "That's nice," or you can use that line, which may or may not be a little test balloon, to show your parent that you're interested in hearing about her friends. You might say, "Where do you know Harry from?" "When was the last time you saw him?" Showing interest will encourage your parent to keep talking.

Go Ahead—Ask!
If you notice that your parent is spending a lot of time with one particular person, speak up and ask about her. Too often adult children think, "If he wanted me to know about the relationship, he'd tell me." But the parent is thinking, "If she were interested in my friend, she'd ask about her." Whether you like this person or not, you can always begin a conversation by saying, "Gloria seems like a nice person. Tell me about her."

Start Talking—It's Never Too Late
If your parent has been dating someone for a while now but you really know nothing about the person, it's not too late to make the first move to open this dialogue. The next time your parent mentions this person's name, grab that as an opportunity to let your parent know you're interested and want to know more. If your parent says something like, "Marie's eldest daughter is going to visit her next week, so we're all going out to dinner at that restaurant I told you

about," keep the dialogue going. Without sounding as though you are interrogating, you can say, "How many children does Marie have?" "Is her family from around here?" Don't assume your parent would have told you these things if he wanted you to know. Maybe he's just waiting for you to ask.

WHAT YOU SHOULD TALK ABOUT

Of course your parent doesn't have to tell you anything at all about her personal life, and you can't decide who she sees or doesn't see. But talking casually with acceptance and love will make her more likely to be open and honest about whom she's seeing. What details of the relationship your parent is willing to share will depend on many factors, but at the very least, let her know that you are willing to listen when she wants to talk.

Breaking the Ice
Talking about your parent's love life is a sensitive subject that you have to broach with care and sensitivity if you want to keep the conversation going. To broach the subject you might

- Begin by talking about your own past relationships.
- Try to include yourself in the relationship.
- Be calm and show interest.

Begin by Talking About Your Own Past Relationships.   There are probably many stories you can recall about growing up with your parents that will help you talk to him now. For instance, there may be times when your parents asked lots of questions about your friends, when they wanted to know what was going on in your life, and when they wanted to help you stay safe and secure. All of these questions grew out of concern and love—the same feelings you want to convey as he now builds new relationships.

You might say: "Hey Mom, remember when I was sixteen and I started dating Eddie? You were forever asking questions about his family and his job and his future goals. I know now that you asked all those questions because you loved me and cared about me. Well, now I see you're dating Sam Smith, and because I love you and care about you, there are some questions I'd like to ask you about him. Would you mind?"

Try to Include Yourself in the Relationship. The best way to get to know someone is to spend time together. Open your home to your parent's friend and try to include him or her in your social plans. This will help establish an ongoing dialogue with your parent.

You might say: "Mom, can you come over for dinner on Sunday? Do you think your friend Roger would like to come too? He's certainly welcome."

You might say: "I have two extra tickets for the concert this weekend. Would you and Sara like to join me? By the way, how are things going with you two?"

Be Calm and Show Interest. As soon as you say something that suggests you don't like your parent's friend, you put your parent in the position of having to defend his decisions and choices. As you broach the subject of your parent's love life, you should be very careful not to sound as though you're accusing him of something bad or that you're badmouthing his friend. You won't find out much about the relationship using these tactics. Instead, if you can react to your parent's introduction of a special friend calmly and with interest (no matter how you really feel), your parent is likely to tell you more and more as time goes on.

Instead of saying: "Mom, why do you spend so much time with Hal? He really doesn't seem your type at all. He's nothing at all like Dad was."

You might say: "Mom, I see that you're spending a lot of time with Hal. I guess the two of you must get along really well. Tell me about him."

Addressing Specific Issues

When your parent is dating someone special, there will undoubtedly be specific issues you'd like to talk to her about that are particular to your family situation. But whatever the topic, if your parent is in good mental health, the guidelines remain the same: as a family member, you can show interest and loving concern, but your parent is an adult who ultimately can do whatever she likes. This section gives you conversation starters for a few common issues that you may want to talk about:

- Your concerns
- Financial leeches
- Overspending
- Extramarital affairs
- Cohabitation
- Prenuptial agreements

Talk About Your Concerns. For the same reasons your parents may not have liked all the people you dated, you may object to their dates. One may drink too much; another may be a flirt; another may be crude and have boorish manners. For uncountable reasons you may not like your parent's companion. The question is: Should you say so? To answer that question, ask yourself how you felt when your parent told you something like, "I just don't like that boy; he's not good enough for you." You may have laughed and did what you wanted anyway, or you may have become angry and closed down all communication; your parent may react the same way, and you'll lose the opportunity to talk. In most cases, it's best to keep your negative opinions to yourself.

However, if you feel that your parent is dating someone who endangers his well-being or safety, then you should voice your concern in a way that is not accusatory if possible. Your goal should be to give your objective point of view and get your parent to rethink the relationship. Always try to avoid a heated debate. In matters of the heart, you cannot bully someone into rational thinking.

You might say: "Remember the time when you caught me with a bottle of wine in my bedroom when I was sixteen? Boy, were you mad, and you grounded me for a month. But I know that was just because you were worried about me. Well, now I guess the tables are turned, because I'm worried about you. I know you enjoy seeing Mr. Jones, but I understand he has a drinking problem. I'm really concerned about that. You know how dangerous drinking and driving is, and although I can't ground you for getting in a car with him, I'm wondering if between the two of us we could figure out a way to keep you safe."

You might say: "Did I tell you that your friend Bob wanted me to bet on the football games last weekend and that then he wanted me to pick a horse for him out of the daily paper? I had a friend like that once who would bet on anything—even things like the weather! Does Bob spend a lot of money feeding this hobby?"

Talk About Financial Leeches.   Your dad is a handsome, accomplished, and wealthy seventy-four-year-old widower. It's no surprise that women of all ages are hanging all over him. Although you know this makes your dad feel pretty special, you also know that some of these women may have more on their minds than just companionship. It's no secret that wealthy seniors are prey for people looking for a free ride and a hefty inheritance. But can you talk to your dad about these ulterior motives without sounding like you're worried about your inheritance? Yes.

The news, the soap operas, and daily conversations give you a springboard for talking about the possibility of an elderly person being taken advantage of. You can tell your parent a story about an elderly person who married a much younger person and then ask, "Do you think it's possible that the younger person is just interested in his money?" See what your parent thinks about this subject. Get a conversation going about the unscrupulous people who prey on the elderly and ask if she has ever met anyone like that. These simple conversations will let you know if your parent is aware that she might easily be a target for financial leeches.

You might say: "Mom, you know I want the best for you. You know I'm not concerned about what I will get from you in your will. That's not an issue to me. What's an issue is your happiness and well-being. I'm wondering how you feel about the possibility that some men looking for some financial security pick up on older widows?"

Talk About Overspending.   Emily's mom had always been a very frugal person. She was the kind who would iron old wrapping paper so it could be used again. This is probably why Emily was so concerned that recently her mom had begun spending a lot of money on her new boyfriend. "She has bought him very expensive gifts, like a TV and a wool overcoat," says Emily. "I know she wants to show how much she appreciates his companionship and attention, but if this keeps up, she's going to go broke very quickly!"

It's natural to want to shower a loved one with gifts, so although you may feel a bit jealous when you hear about the latest gift your parent has bought her beau, all you can really do is nod and smile—unless, that is, the gifts are truly extravagant and you worry about your parent's financial security. Then it's time to have a talk.

You might say: "Dad, I think it's really good that you have found someone to go out with. You and Bertha really have a good time, don't you? My concern is the way this social life might affect you financially in the long run. You've worked hard all your life to make sure you'd be financially set in your retirement; I know that's very important to you. But when you go on these expensive vacations and buy expensive gifts, you may end up short on cash very soon. If that happens, you know I'd try to help you the best I can, but I don't have that much myself. Have you thought about this?"

Talk About Extramarital Affairs. Although you may wish your widowed parent companionship and happiness, you may be surprised to find that the new flame is still married. This is especially likely to be the case for females, due to the fact that there just aren't many unmarried elderly men around! A profile of older Americans compiled by AARP found that there are five times as many widows (8.6 million) as widowers (1.7 million). And that whereas only 43 percent of older women are married, a whopping 76 percent of older men are married. The odds are certainly against finding an elderly available male.

This was the case for sixty-nine-year-old Margaret. She had been dating Fred for the past year, knowing from the start that he was married. Her daughter, Monica, was happy for her and was even somewhat relieved that there was someone else to keep her mother busy and happy. But that was before she found out he was married. Then Monica turned on Fred. She told her mother she was a fool to stay with him and that Fred was no longer welcome in her home. "I can't believe this man has been out dancing with my mother," cried Monica, "while his wife lies sick in a nursing home bed. I think that says something about his character, and I'd really like my mother to dump him."

This is not an uncommon scenario. Fred's wife has been in a nursing home for five years. She no longer recognizes him and is often barely conscious. He visits her regularly and pays her medical bills, but his life without her has been very lonely. When Fred met Margaret, she was a warm and gracious person he could talk to, and without planning to, he fell in love with her. This is a tough situa-tion that does technically make Fred's relationship with Margaret adulterous. Certainly, both Fred and Margaret have talked about the awkwardness of the situation, but they have decided to follow their hearts and continue their relationship. Unfortunately, Monica's reaction (which admittedly is based on the values and morals taught to her by her mother!) will alienate her from her mother. This is something they need to talk about before the communication gap grows too wide to cross.

You might say: "Mom, you know I think Bill is a really nice person, but it's hard for me to feel good about your relationship because he's married. Can you talk to me about how you feel about the situation? Maybe you can help me better understand why you're dating him."

Talk About Cohabitation.   Back when your parents were growing up, cohabitation was unheard of among older Americans; in fact, it was practically nonexistent at any age. But today things have changed: the number of cohabiting adults age fifty-five and over has doubled in the last ten years, reaching more than one million. How will you feel and what will you say if your parent decides to become part of this change by living with a "significant other" and choosing not to marry? For some this situation is welcomed, but for others it is shocking and causes much family upset.

Whether you love the idea or hate it, before you give your opinion you should give your congratulations, remembering that your parent is an adult who can make adult decisions without your permission. You should also look past your own emotional reaction and consider why your parent may have made this decision. Some older couples avoid marriage to avoid the financial entanglements. Some don't want to mix finances for inheritance reasons. Others worry that remarriage will prompt increased taxation on their Social Security income or a reduction or elimination of public assistance or private pension survivor benefits. And many worry about the high cost of long-term care that could wipe out their savings if they were married and their partner became ill.

There are also many cohabiting older couples who simply don't want to get married. Some may have had bad experiences in the past. Some may not want to make a legal commitment for a variety of reasons. And some simply want companionship but don't see the point of a late-life marriage.

Your parent doesn't owe you an explanation, but because a new living arrangement is certainly a big part of his or her life, it's a subject you should feel free to talk about—if you can do it without shutting the doors of communications with anger or accusations.

Instead of saying: "Why would you do this? It is a really bad idea."
You might say: "I'm not sure I understand why you are doing this. Tell me about it."

Instead of saying: "I don't think you know what you're getting in to."
You might say: "I'm sure you've thought about this a long time. Let's talk about how this will change things for you—both for better and for worse."

Instead of saying: "Why, you sexy guy. I didn't know you had that much energy left in you."
You might say: "I'm very happy for you. I'm glad you've found someone who makes you feel loved."

Talk About Prenuptial Agreements.   When an elderly person marries, should the new spouse—who may have known the new partner for only a short time—be entitled to inherit all the family assets at the time of divorce or the spouse's death? This is a question that your family may want to talk about, especially if your parent is bringing the lion's share of wealth into the new marriage. Because prenuptial agreements are not something with which people of your parent's generation may be very familiar or comfortable, you may want to talk about these arrangements—if only to introduce the idea and give your parent something to think about.

Drawing up a prenuptial agreement is an appropriate legal step to take before exchanging vows—especially with elderly people who have worked their whole lives to build up a financial base to support themselves and their children. It's difficult to sound concerned rather than greedy, but the point should be made that this is an issue to consider.

You might say: "Before you marry Gwyn, I was wondering if you two have talked about a prenuptial agreement. I know that sounds kind of unromantic, but it's something you should look into. Many prenuptials for elderly couples simply state that each person will keep whatever he or she initially brought to the marriage in the event of divorce or death. You know I love Gwyn; I'm only making a suggestion that at the same time you should protect yourself from the unknown in the future."

When you talk to your parent about a new romance, make it positive and upbeat so she will want to continue the dialogue. Make her feel comfortable. Give her positive feedback and reinforcement. Be a supporter. If this person gives your parent comfort and happiness and no one is going to get hurt, give the couple your blessing.

EXPERT HELP

This chapter has been prepared with the expert help of Paul A. Falzone, president and CEO of The Right One, a personal introduction service. Based in Hingham, Massachusetts, The Right One has offices in twenty-two states.

Geriatric Care Managers

One of the major pluses of having a geriatric care manager look after the affairs of the elderly is that it takes an enormously difficult task off the shoulders of the adult children.

> *Alice J. Kethley, Ph.D., executive director of the Benjamin Rose Institute*

Maryann knew her eighty-one-year-old mother was a little shaky on her feet and that she was sometimes forgetful, but she wasn't expecting the call she received one evening from the manager of the apartment complex where her mother lived. He told Maryann that her mother had fallen once again and that he was not comfortable with her living alone in the apartment any longer. Of course he was concerned about the liability of the situation, but he was also concerned for this woman who was living alone in an apartment that was not set up to accommodate the needs of elderly people. Maryann was very worried about her mother, but living out-of-state made it difficult to care for her as she wanted to.

The next morning Maryann flew to her mother's side in New Orleans and tried to convince her to leave her apartment and move in with her. When her mother refused even to consider that idea, Maryann called the National Association of Geriatric Care Managers looking for some guidance. The care manager quickly arranged to have her mom's health and needs evaluated over the next few days while Maryann was still in town. Soon they learned that Maryann's mom was in the early stages of Alzheimer's and that if she wanted to stay out of a nursing home she would need in-home health care. Maryann and her mom agreed that such care would be very helpful and asked the care manager to make the arrangements.

This care manager immediately brought in the home care aide, monitored her work, and kept in touch with Maryann after Maryann returned to her own home. The care manager also visited Maryann's mom each week to make sure she had everything she needed and to keep an eye on her physical and mental health.

Over the next few months, the care manager recommended changes as she saw that they became necessary. First she increased the daytime home care to round-the-clock care and then ultimately recommended a transfer to a nursing home as she saw the mother's cognitive skills declining. This geriatric care manager still monitors Maryann's mother's care at the nursing home and still reports back to Maryann each week. "As long as the care manager is looking after my mother's needs and her care," says Maryann, "I can rest at night. I don't know what I would do without her."

Geriatric care managers (GCMs) are helping thousands and thousands of families cope with the long-term care of elderly parents. These professionals often have training in gerontology, social work, nursing, or counseling. They also have extensive knowledge about the cost, quality, and availability of services in an older person's community. As a result, GCMs can perform the following services:

- Conduct care-planning assessments to identify problems and determine the need for services and eligibility for assistance
- Screen, arrange, and monitor in-home help or other services
- Review financial, legal, or medical issues and offer referrals to geriatric specialists to avoid future problems and conserve assets
- Provide crisis intervention
- Act as a liaison to families living away from the parent, making sure things are going well and alerting families to problems
- Help move an older person to or from a retirement complex, nursing home, or other care facility
- Provide consumer education and advocacy
- Offer counseling and support

Many elderly individuals could benefit from these services if they knew they existed and how to find them. It's a good idea to talk to your parents about the possibility of finding and retaining a GCM if the need should arise. This chapter gives you some guidelines that will help you know when your parents might need a GCM. It gives you the words you need to broach the subject and address specific aspects of geriatric care. And it offers tips to help you locate and hire a qualified care manager.

WHY TALK ABOUT
GERIATRIC CARE MANAGERS

Do you know what federal, state, and local services your parents are entitled to as senior citizens? Do you know if they are receiving all the health benefits they are eligible for? Do you know how they are managing their money? Do you know if they need help getting to and from their appointments or getting out of the tub? Do you know for sure if they can manage their daily activities without help? It is difficult for even the most involved family member to know the answers to these kinds of questions. The rights, benefits, and needs of the elderly are many and complex, and your parents may need the help of someone who is trained to know these things.

Although this book can guide you through conversations you might have with your parents about really important things, it cannot give you all the information you need to be able to effectively handle the financial, legal, health, and personal issues of elder care. GCMs are trained to do this. A trained GCM can also be a valued intermediary between you and your parents when you need to discuss things like moving, finances, stopping driving, cognitive health, personal health, or hiring a home care worker. When *you* bring up these issues, your parents may tune out all the facts and hear only the message that you think they're too old to take of themselves. If you have a care manager working with your parents, they are more likely to listen to this professional who is trained to deal with the different aspects of elder care.

This was the case for Ed and his parents. Ed is a lawyer who was well aware of the services available to his elderly parents and who could easily navigate them through the system—if only they would listen to him. Ed had tried for several years to convince his father to get medical help for his mother, who seemed to have some mental and emotional problems. The father dismissed the idea completely and refused to talk about it. In desperation, Ed finally hired a GCM to talk to his parents and to assess if his mom needed medical care. The care manager recognized the signs of early dementia and recommended, as did Ed, that Ed's mom have a physical examination by her doctor. Surprisingly, both parents agreed that that would be a good idea. (The care manager laughs when she admits that she suggested nothing that Ed hadn't already begged them to do!) The care manager got the mom involved in a geriatric assessment program and personally brought her to appointments with her family physician and then a neurologist. She then handpicked a home aide, who is now working in their home five days a week to help Ed's mom with her activities of daily living.

If you believe that your parents need assistance that you cannot give them (or that they won't let you give), you should talk to them about the possibility of hiring a GCM.

WHEN TO TALK ABOUT GERIATRIC CARE MANAGERS

Marjorie's family sat down to talk about hiring a GCM to help handle her finances when she received a notice from the IRS demanding $4,000 in unpaid taxes. Jake's family gathered to talk about finding a GCM when he collapsed from uncontrolled high blood pressure after forgetting to renew his prescription. Gilda's family saw the need for a care manager when she signed a contract agreeing to leave her home to a neighbor after her death.

Most commonly the subject of a GCM comes up after crises like these—when it is indisputable that an elderly person can no longer handle his or her personal, financial, medical, or legal affairs alone. In these situations, hiring a care manager is often a necessity thrust upon the elderly whether they like it or not, and the choice of care manager is made in a hurry, without enough care given to the screening process. The middle of a crisis is not the ideal time to talk about hiring a GCM.

It is much easier on everyone involved when the subject of a GCM is discussed and settled before a crisis. This is a subject that can be talked about in conversation long before a care manager is actually needed. The term can be introduced in casual conversations about other people and about senior services in general. Then, if down the road there is a need for help, the idea is not something brand-new and doesn't seem as threatening.

Other times you should think about finding a geriatric care manager include the following:

- When you don't have the time, money, or know-how to look after all the needs of your elderly parents. You may be too wrapped up in your own family and your own children's needs to have the emotional energy to give full-time attention to the needs of your parents.
- When you feel guilty that you are in some ways abandoning your parents because you can't look after all their affairs, yet you simply don't have the resources to do it all.
- When your parents do not agree with your recommendations or advice about how their legal, financial, or personal affairs should be handled, yet you're sure that they are incapable of making sound decisions themselves.
- When friends, relatives, doctors, or other professionals say to you that they think your parents may need some help.
- When you feel you do not have an objective view of your par-

ents' true needs. This can happen when professionals (or your gut) suggest that your parents can no longer think clearly about all their affairs, but you resist believing they could be suffering some form of dementia. Or it can happen when you live away from your parents and are not able to fairly judge their mental and physical health.

WHAT YOU SHOULD TALK ABOUT

Talking about a GCM with elderly parents can be like walking a tightrope: one wrong word and the issue is dead. It's best to explore your parents' needs, slowly break the ice, and then address specific issues.

Talking to Others First

Before you bring up the subject of GCMs, it's a good idea to get the facts by talking to others who are close to your parents. If you do not live in your parents' house, you may not be sufficiently involved in your parents' lives to know for sure if they are capable of handling their own affairs. As the adult child, you may not be objective enough to know when your parents need help. If you live a distance away from your parents, you may not know half of what's going on and will need the input of those closer to your parents. These others may include their religious minister, their physician, and close friends.

If Zach had asked, anyone in Martha's neighborhood could have told him that his mother needed help. Zach called his mother faithfully every Sunday night, and every Sunday night she assured him that she was just fine. But in her close-knit community, the neighbors had been noticing for quite some time that Martha was just not herself. They saw her walking around her yard in her pajamas many late afternoons. They saw her begin to wander in the middle of the night. She seemed to be losing weight, and her appearance was disheveled. They would bring her back home when she was out late at night. They would close the front door that she often left wide open. They brought her nutritious meals on special occasions. But eventually her next-door neighbor felt that Martha needed professional help. Not knowing how to contact her son, the neighbor called the police to ask for advice. They referred him to the state's Adult Protection Service, which called in a geriatric care case manager. This person was able to find Martha's out-of-state son and then arranged for Martha's physical and neurological evaluation and ultimately for twenty-four-hour in-home care. This story ended happily, but Martha could have been supported much sooner if her son had just asked around.

When you talk to friends and neighbors, it's not necessary to say, "Do you think I should hire a geriatric care manager for my father?" By posing general questions, you'll get the information you need without setting off the crisis alarm.

You might say: "I worry so much about my father living alone. I want to make sure he has everything he needs and is always able to get supportive services if he wants them. How do you think he's doing?"

Another person you might check with is your parents' accountant (oddly enough), if they have one. These professionals see the deficits and losses and will notice when financial mistakes are being made. They know when unusual and out-of-the-ordinary purchases are made. They see when an elderly person has been scammed. They know when the rent hasn't been paid. They know when overdrafts become commonplace.

You might say: "I worry about my parents being alone and misman-aging their finances. I'd like you to tell me if you notice any red flags that might indicate that they may need some help."

Breaking the Ice

Ideally, you will have conversations with your parents about GCMs long before they actually need one. If you do, you can talk about this service in a very general way. None of these conversations have to be about your own parents at all. The idea is to take away the shame or stigma that some elderly associate with being "managed." There are many ways you can break the ice on this subject. For starters, you can talk about

- Other people who need long-term care
- The growth of the industry
- The value of having help and support
- A neutral third party

Talk About Other People Who Need Long-Term Care. To familiarize your parents with the concept of GCMs, use the term in conversation long before one is actually needed.

You might say: "My friend Mary has an elderly mother whom she loves dearly. She worries, though, that her mother may have trou-ble living alone and keeping track of all the complex services and entitlements for senior citizens. So she just hired a geriatric care manager to help and support her mother. Have you ever heard of this kind of professional?"

Talk About the Growth of the Industry. As the population ages, the geriatric care business is booming. In a simple conversation about business and the economy, you can discuss this industry and the services it provides.

You might say: "I was reading the other day about this geriatric care company that has opened in my state. The article said that these companies are offering services to senior citizens who need some help keeping track of their personal, medical, financial, and legal rights and responsibilities. Do you think this kind of company will succeed?"

Talk About the Value of Having Help and Support.   When you first discuss this subject with your parents, do not say, "You need a geriatric care manager." People in general object to being "managed." (Also, the growth and problems of the managed care health insurance industry have added to the stigma of the term *care manager* as someone whose job it is to make sure you don't get what you need unless you're in a crisis.) Instead of talking about care management, talk about the value of getting help and support.

You might say: "There are so many laws today giving older people services, benefits, and privileges that it's hard to keep track of them all to make sure you're getting what you're entitled to. I think these care managers who give help and support to the elderly and look out for their rights are a good idea. What do you think?"

Talk About a Neutral Third Party.   Your parents may not like being told by you that they need help, but they may not be offended by advice or help that comes from a local university or their place of worship.

You might say: "I was talking to the pastor of your church the other day, and he asked how you were doing. He told me about a service that might help and support you, so I looked into it, and here's what I found."

Addressing Specific Issues

Asking your parents to hire a GCM is asking them to agree that they can no longer take care of their own affairs—that's a tough subject to talk about. When you're ready to sit down and talk about the specific details, always be sensitive to their feelings and the role reversal that may make them feel uncomfortable and even defensive.

Encourage your parents to see the care manager as a helping hand, not as a sign of incapacity or of being abandoned. Emphasize that keeping track of the financial, legal, personal, and health aspects of life is tough for everyone.

You might say: "I just finished doing my bills, and I sure wish there were someone who could keep all these financial and legal matters in order for me. There just seem to be so many things to keep track of. Lots of senior citizens are fortunate to get this kind of help from someone who understands the complicated care system for seniors—things like taxes, Social Security, and insurance. In fact, I've been thinking that someone like this could give you a lot of support and take a load off your mind. I've been talking to such a person, named Kathleen Smith, who I'd like to introduce you to next Monday. Is four o'clock a good time?"

If your parent asks for help that you can't give, this is an opportunity to broach the subject of a caregiver. When you can't do it, offer help from someone who can.

You might say: "I'd love to do this for you, but I just can't. But I do know that there are people who are trained to understand the public and private systems that provide services, support, and entitlements to the older population. I'm going to get the details for you, and we'll look into this service."

You should also discuss the cost. If your parents are on Medicaid, they already have a caseworker assigned to manage their care. But if your parents are not on Medicaid, they are probably on their own, and most insurance companies do not pay for GCMs. If your parents resist paying for this service when you know they need it and can afford it, you can try to encourage them to see the value of the service. (Of course if your parents cannot afford this care but you feel it is necessary, you can offer to pay for it yourself.)

You might say: "What is the price of peace of mind? This is an expense that will give you the freedom to enjoy your life without worrying about every little detail of a very complex system."

GET THE FACTS

If you feel your parents do need a GCM, help them do the legwork. Older people who need this kind of help don't have the psychological energy to search out the appropriate places and people who offer geriatric care. You will find it a bit daunting yourself and will understand why it's not something you can throw out to your parents as a good idea they should look into on their own.

Finding a good GCM takes time and effort. The field of geriatric care management is relatively unregulated, and many people without specialized training identify themselves as care managers, care coordinators, or care advisers. Often licensed social workers or nurses enter into the business of geriatrics without any further training; some of them are wonderful, whereas others are not equipped to work with the elderly.

Referrals through family and friends are the best way to find a competent GCM. A strong recommendation from someone who has firsthand experience with the care worker gives you much peace of mind. If you cannot get a personal recommendation, you might try these other sources of information:

- Your local university. If it has a center on aging, people in this department may be able to refer you to a reputable geriatric care company.
- Church-related organizations such as Jewish Family Services and Catholic Charities. They often make referrals.
- Your parents' place of worship. Many religious leaders know a lot about elder care and can guide you in the right direction.
- The Visiting Nurse Service in your parents' area.
- The Area Agency on Aging in your parents' community.
- Hospitals, senior centers, and geriatric assessment centers.
- Any of the organizations listed in the Resources at the end of this chapter.

When screening care managers, ask about their training, education, and background in care management and geriatrics. Although there are no licensing requirements for GCMs, there are certification programs. Ask the candidates you interview if they are certified and by whom. Also check to see if they belong to the National Association of Professional Geriatric Care Managers or any other professional associations (and then double-check with the association to be sure). You might ask the following questions:

- How long have you been a care manager?
- What are your credentials?
- What hours are you available?
- Do you provide home care services?
- How will you keep in touch with me?
- Can you provide references?
- What are your fees? Do you have them in writing?

When you talk to your parents about finding and retaining a GCM, you should be very sensitive to their fears and need for independence. You cannot arrive one day and announce that you have hired a GCM to take care of them. This is a life-changing decision that needs to be talked about and mutually agreed on.

RESOURCES

National Association of Professional Geriatric Care Managers
1604 North Country Club Road
Tucson, AZ 85716
(520) 881-8008
www.caremanager.org

National Council on the Aging
409 Third Street SW, Suite 200
Washington, DC 20024
(202) 479-1200
www.ncoa.org

Case Management Society of America
8201 Cantrell Road, Suite 230
Little Rock, AR 72227
(501) 225-2229

Eldercare Locator
(800) 677-1116 (weekdays 9 A.M. to 8 P.M. EST)
www.aoa.gov/elderpage/locator.html

This service offers a national toll-free number staffed by representatives who direct callers to the best source of information on services for the elderly in a local community.

EXPERT HELP

This chapter was written with the expert help of two individuals. Alice J. Kethley, Ph.D., executive director of the Benjamin Rose Institute in Cleveland, Ohio. This is a nonprofit agency that delivers social, health, and residential services to the elderly and their families. Dr. Kethley is nationally renowned in the field of aging, having recently served as chair of the National Chronic Care Consortium and as president of the American Society on Aging.

Dianne Boazman, LCSW, CMC, is president of the National Association of Geriatric Care Managers (NAGCM). This is a nonprofit professional organization of practitioners whose goal is the advancement of dignified care for the elderly and their families. With more than one thousand members, the NAGCM is committed to maximizing the independence and autonomy of elders while striving to ensure that the highest quality and most cost-effective health and human services are used when and where appropriate.

Part Two

Mental Health

Grief and Bereavement

People experiencing a great loss need to go through a grieving process in which they have to get worse before they get better. Talking to someone about the emotional pain is the best way to get through a difficult time.

> Michael H. Beechem, MSW, Ph.D., *director of the Center on Aging at the University of West Florida*

It took seventy-seven-year-old Colonel Brian White almost fifty years to learn the importance of talking about grief. When Brian was eleven years old, his father committed suicide, and no one in his family, including his mother, three siblings, and an uncle, would discuss the death because they felt too ashamed and hurt. This began Brian's life of silent grieving.

At the age of twenty-one, Brian was commissioned as an Air Force officer. Following the necessary flight training, he became a pilot in World War II and was sent to Europe, where he flew several combat missions into Germany. Four of his close friends, fellow pilots, were killed in combat, and again his support system discouraged expressions of grief. "Death denial," he says, "was a coping strategy we all used to survive the war." He also says that the letters from his mother and siblings never acknowledged the emotional pain he tried to express in his letters home.

Following the war, Brian became a career officer and married, but life was not easy for him. He suffered flashbacks involving the death of his friends, and his wife would grow angry when he tried to talk about his feelings of grief. "Leave it in the past," she would say. "Don't let yourself get worked up about something you can't do anything about."

Over the following forty years, Brian divorced twice and lost track of his three children. He became depressed and started drinking heavily. He did seek the help of an Air Force physician once, who told him the flashbacks would go away in time and that his drinking probably "did more good than harm."

Then, after thirty years of military service, Brian retired and finally decided to seek help for his depression. At the age of sixty-two, he found a therapist who allowed him to tell his story. He was given permission to express the strong feelings associated with his unresolved issues of loss and grief, and this made all the difference in his life.

Today Colonel White is seventy-seven years old with fifteen years of sobriety behind him. He has become very active as a volunteer for the local chapter of the Council on Aging, where he feels he can help others "simply by letting them talk about the things that hurt them emotionally."

Colonel White's story is a clear illustration of why it's so important to allow our elderly parents to talk about their feelings of grief. When your parent loses a spouse, a sibling, a dear friend, or even a beloved pet, he or she will naturally feel the pain and sorrow of profound grief. Of course you will offer what words of comfort you can at the time, but it's important to remember that the grieving period does not end with the funeral. Grief is a rather lengthy process, but it takes more than time: there must also be lots of open communication and an ever-patient and empathic ear.

WHY TALK ABOUT GRIEF

It is well known that talking about feelings is absolutely vital to working through the grieving process. What might be called "talking therapy" allows a person to verbalize pain. It gives the body an outlet for hurt and anger. It helps one organize thoughts and feelings that can get confused and muddled during the grieving process.

Unfortunately, people of our parents' generation are usually uncomfortable talking about feelings or admitting "weaknesses." Many don't want to be a burden, and they don't want to be perceived as dependent, so they repress their feelings and will always say, "I'm fine" but then pay the price in mental and physical illnesses.

Joe didn't know this, so when his father didn't mention any problems after his wife of sixty years died of a sudden heart attack, Joe assumed all was well. "Actually," says Joe, "I expected that my father would be devastated after Mom's death because he was very dependent on her for everything. But he really seemed just fine.

When we talked on the phone he would tell me about his fishing adventures and movies he had seen. I thought he was doing a good job keeping himself busy and upbeat."

But then Joe dropped by to visit unexpectedly, and he knew right away that something was very wrong. The house was a disaster: old newspapers, dirty dishes, and lots of garbage littered the floors and tables. Joe found his dad sitting in a darkened corner. He was unshaven and had lost weight. His clothes were soiled and crumpled. Apparently he had not been out of the house at all in the two weeks since his wife died; he had made up those stories to keep his son from worrying about him. "I felt just awful," remembers Joe. "I should never have left him alone all that time." When Joe went over and knelt down by him, his dad pulled him close and began to sob. "It was the first time in my life I had ever seen him cry. I had no idea what to do for him."

Joe didn't know it at the time, but just by being there, by letting his father cry, and by empathizing with his father's pain he was doing a great deal of good for his father. The fact is, if grief is not recognized and talked about, the predictable outcome is depression—sometimes even clinical depression that may require intensive psychotherapy and medications.

It's important to let your parent know that talking about her feelings is not putting a burden on you. Let her know you're glad to listen.

WHEN TO TALK ABOUT GRIEF

You can talk to your parent about his feelings of grief anytime at all without worrying that you'll open old wounds. It's not true that bringing up the subject will only hurt more and prolong the healing time. In fact, the more often he can verbalize how he feels, the faster he will heal. That's why you should plan to talk to your parent about his feelings

- At the time of immediate grief
- As often and for as long as it takes

At the Time of Immediate Grief

It's so hard to know what to say to someone who has just experienced a very painful loss. You say, "I'm sorry"; you say, "I know how bad you must feel." But then what? Very often there is nothing more to say, and so we turn our conversation to the weather or sports, hoping this will help take the grieving person's mind off his or her pain.

The truth is that the pain is still there even when someone is talking about the weather—it's just hidden for the moment. But it will be back. May knew her mother was grieving deeply after her dog died. May's mother is a widow living alone; Kip was her sole companion for fifteen years, and this loss was surely devastating. But her mother was putting up a brave front and would chatter on and on about anything but the dog. "I knew if I mentioned Kip's name she would start crying, and I didn't want her to hurt more than she already did," reasoned May. "Every time I'd get ready to ask her how she was feeling, she'd launch into another story about something else. I figured this was her way of dealing with it, so we never talked about that loss at all."

Yes, if you bring up the subject of your parent's loss, he may cry. That's OK—in fact it's good. Experts know that if we don't cry and mourn our losses they are much harder to get over. So a good time to talk about feelings of grief is when you know your parent is grieving.

As Often and For as Long as It Takes

If you sit down with your parent after a loss and actively listen and talk empathically, you have done a good thing—but that shouldn't be the end of the discussion. Grief is something that goes on for a long time, and the grieving person needs permission to air her grief and be supported for however long it takes. That's why being truly supportive of someone experiencing grief requires a great deal of patience.

Bob had had it with his mother. His father had died three months ago, and she still cried about it every time he saw her. "It's to the point," he says, "where I don't even want to call her on the phone because I know she's just going to start crying again. I know she misses him, but enough is enough. It's time to move on. I'm going to tell her that if she wants me to call her she has to stop talking about Dad."

If Bob insists that his mother stop mourning her husband, she'll probably stop crying to Bob, but that won't stop the grieving. In fact, it will make it much harder for her to make a healthy recovery. Unfortunately, we live in a fast-paced society that tolerates people's expressions of the pain of grieving for only a short while. If someone seems to be dragging out the process by grieving "too long," we become impatient and close off all opportunities to talk "again" about how much it hurts.

Commonly, people fear that if they let someone go on and on about how sad he feels, he'll never get over it. This just isn't the case. If your parent is able to put his grief into words, you are helping him work through these feelings if you continue to be supportive and empathic for as long as it takes.

WHAT YOU SHOULD TALK ABOUT

What can you say that will make someone who is grieving feel better? The words are hard to find. Most often, it's not what you say but what you invite your parent to say that is most healing. When you talk with your parent about her loss, think about the guidelines covered in this section:

Breaking the Ice

When you talk to your parents about their emotional pain, try to remember that no one can really understand what someone else's grief feels like. You will be most helpful if you ease into a conversation on this subject with sensitivity and empathy. To break the ice, you might try these communication tips:

- Don't patronize
- Start with feelings

Don't Patronize. "You'll be OK, Mom. Don't cry." These words of reassurance are the ones that come most naturally when we try to help someone deal with grief. Unfortunately, they can easily be misunderstood because they can imply that the loss is not that great. You may not actually say, "Snap out of it," but reassurances can sound like that. Saying "You'll feel much better soon; you're strong and will be just fine" diminishes what your grieving parent is feeling. It sounds as though you're making light of the experience. So think twice before you reassure your grieving parent.

There are a few other "don'ts" you should keep in mind when consoling your mom or dad:

Don't lecture: "You have to be strong and go on with your life."
Don't sermonize: "Dad wouldn't want you to spend your days crying like this."
Don't be judgmental: "You're not even trying to get over this."

Start with Feelings.   Although it's hard to find the right words to help a parent who is in emotional pain, you can't go wrong if you always speak with empathy—try to imagine how that person is feeling and echo that feeling back to him. This will work whether you're talking about emotions, physical pain, the stages of grief, or even abnormal grieving.

Instead of saying: "Don't cry; it'll be OK."
You might say: "This must be very painful for you."

Instead of saying: "It's time for you to get on with your life."
You might say: "Down the road, you will have happy days again, but I understand how difficult this is for you right now."

Instead of saying: "She had been very sick; this is really a blessing."
You might say: "Although she is finally out of pain, I know you must miss her terribly."

Instead of saying: "He lived a long life; no one can go on forever."
You might say: "I know he lived a long, good life, but it is still difficult to accept."

Addressing Specific Issues
There are certain issues that your parents might want or need to discuss. Here are a few to help you encourage heart-to-heart communication. You might talk

- Through the stages of grief
- About possible hypochondria
- Without saying a word
- About abnormal grief

Talk Through the Stages of Grief. It's important to keep the lines of communication open through all the various stages of grief. In her book *On Death and Dying*, Elisabeth Kübler-Ross identified five stages of grief: (1) denial and isolation, (2) anger, (3) bargaining, (4) depression, and (5) acceptance. Almost all of us pass through all five stages during times of great loss, though not necessarily in any specific order and sometimes through more than one stage simultaneously or by jumping back and forth from one to another. If you keep your empathic antennae up, you'll notice which stage your parent is experiencing at a particular time, and you can focus a supportive conversation on her needs at that stage. The following are possible ways to open a conversation that will show her that you are still open to talking about her feelings and are willing to listen if she needs to talk.

Denial and Isolation. If your parent is suffering through denial and isolation, she may intellectually know her loved one is dead, but she hasn't accepted that fact emotionally and has trouble dealing with the reality of the outer world.

You might say: "Sometimes I feel like Dad is going to just walk right through that door and sit down and have a cup of coffee with me. It's so hard to accept his death. Do you ever feel like that?"

You might say: "Sometimes when I think about Mom dying, I just want to be alone. Do you feel like that?"

You might say: "I know it's hard to imagine life without Dad, but soon we'll adjust to his loss and hold on to our wonderful memories."

Anger.   If your parent is experiencing feelings of anger, you should remind yourself that most often the anger is misplaced. If, for example, he feels abandoned by your deceased mother, he may lash out at you when you call to say hello. It takes much patience and understanding to recognize what's going on and not to respond with anger of your own.

You might say (calmly, without anger): "I know you're feeling angry, but instead of yelling at me, I think you need to figure out exactly what you're angry at. Maybe your anger has more to do with feeling sad about Mom's death. Have you thought about that?"

Bargaining.   If your parent begins bargaining to save the life of a terminally ill loved one—"If he lives, I promise I'll dedicate the rest of my life to raising money to find a cure for this illness" or "If the Lord spares his life, I will dedicate my life to doing good deeds"—don't throw cold water on the idea, but don't lose sight of reality either. (Most often these "deals" are silent and private, but if your parent should talk about this aloud, don't rush to judgment.)

You might say: "That's a noble offer, Mom. Even if Dad dies, that would still be a very good idea."

Depression.   If your parent is dealing with depression caused by grief, be sure to read the next chapter, "Depression," to help you find the right words to ease the mental pain.

Acceptance.   When your parent reaches the stage of acceptance, she will finally feel peaceful and calm. It may seem unnecessary to say anything now that things have finally settled down, but in your continuing dialogue about grief, it's nice to let your parent know that you're still nearby if she wants to talk.

You might say: "Mom, I've noticed that you seem a bit happier and more peaceful lately. I'm glad that you've been able to work through your sad feelings about Mary's death. But I want you to know that if you ever want to talk about her, you can always give me a call. I love hearing those stories about the two of you."

Talk About Possible Hypochondria.   Obsession with personal health is common after the death of a loved one. If your parent had been in good health until the loss and now has constant medical complaints that his doctor cannot find cause for, you can help him see the true source by simply offering food for thought, without requiring a confession.

Rather than say: "Cut it out; there is nothing wrong with you."
You might say: "Why do you think your doctor can't find a cause for this medical problem?"

You might say: "I've heard that stress can cause real physical problems like the ones you have. Maybe your backache and sore throat will go away when you've had more time to get over the death of your sister."

You might say: "I see you're taking care of yourself with a good diet, and your doctor has given you a clean bill of health. Have you thought that maybe your medical complaints are simply your body's way of dealing with your feelings of loss and grief?"

Talk Without Saying a Word.   You can also help your parent talk about feelings by being an active listener. This is one time when you

don't have to do all the talking—you can best communicate with
your parent by letting her do the talking—and letting her know you
are willing to listen. Even if she moans on for months and months—
keep listening.

Talk About Abnormal Grief.   If you feel your parent's grief is
excessive and possibly abnormal, you need to talk to him about ways
to find help. The symptoms of abnormal grief are not entirely different from normal grief; it is a matter of degree. Although normal
grief causes changes in appetite, sleeping habits, and other behaviors, abnormal grief shows itself in extremes of behavior: eating too
much or not at all, sleeping too much or not at all, talking incessantly or completely withdrawing, being extremely hostile or totally
apathetic. If these extremes continue for a prolonged period, it's time
to talk about getting help. This is difficult, because most people
become very defensive when a loved one touches on the subject of
mental health. The problem is compounded because, in general,
people of our parents' generation are not open to the idea of psychotherapy or counseling.

You might say: "Dad, I'm worried about you. I know you're finding it
difficult to live without Mom and that sometimes it seems like you'll
never get over her loss. I'd like to help you get help dealing with
your feelings."

You might say: "Mom, it's important to me that you have a good
life—even without the companionship and love of your dog. Have
you noticed that since his death you haven't been out of your house
much at all and that you really aren't eating right? I'd like to help
you get past these painful feelings. Let's make an appointment to
visit your doctor."

You might say: "There are so many people your age who also have lost a loved one who might feel better after talking to you and knowing that someone understands their pain. You know exactly how they feel. In fact, there is a group that meets every Tuesday afternoon at the church on Main Street. Why don't you go and see what it's all about?"

Grief is a very personal and private experience. But if you can help your parents give words to their emotional pain you give them something that is priceless as they struggle to live through this difficult time.

RESOURCE

For twenty-five years, the self-help program of AARP, the Widowed Persons Service, has been widely recognized in the bereavement community as a national self-help organization that effectively assists widowed persons through the grieving process. In communities throughout the nation, trained widowed volunteers working with local AARP programs offer the newly widowed and others the following services:

- One-to-one outreach
- Group meetings, including support groups, educational meetings, guest speakers, and online discussion groups
- Publications and training materials on bereavement
- Referrals to community resources
- Social activities

To locate the closest AARP Widowed Persons Service program, call (800) 424-3410 or e-mail griefandloss@aarp.org.

EXPERT HELP

This chapter was written with the expert help of Michael H. Beechem, MSW, Ph.D., director of the Center on Aging at the University of West Florida in Pensacola, Florida. Dr. Beechem's expertise lies in the fields of gerontology and grief therapy. He is an expert on helping people cope with loss. He has written for *Hospice Journal,* a magazine published for the elderly, concerning the grieving process. Dr. Beechem can be reached at (850) 474-2376 or at mbeechem@uwf.edu.

Depression

If you see signs of depression, you should talk to your parents about your suspicions, because depression is a treatable, physical illness—every bit as real as cancer and heart disease.

Patrick Mathiasen, M.D.,
author of Late Life Depression

"What is the matter with me?" eighty-two-year-old Marge asked her daughter, Mary Ellen. "I went for a medical checkup just last week and the doctor says I'm fine, but I don't think he knows what he's talking about. I feel so achy and tired that I just want to cry!" Mary Ellen assured her mom that the doctor was a caring and knowledgeable man who couldn't do anything about the normal aches and pains of aging. "You are getting a little older now, Mom," Mary Ellen kidded her mother. "It's natural to feel less energetic and fit."

In fact, Mary Ellen was worried. Her mother had never been one to complain and had always been a very independent go-getter. But lately she just wasn't herself. She looked run down; she was awfully irritable and kept insisting that she couldn't sleep and that her whole body ached. But not wanting to worry her mother further, Mary Ellen tried to cheer her up. "Why don't we go out for a good lunch and do a little shopping? I'll bet that will make you feel much better."

Maybe an afternoon with her daughter is just what Marge needs to start feeling better, but it's more likely that she needs prompt medical attention from someone who knows the signs and symptoms of depression. Depression is a disease that touches all ages, but it is especially prevalent in the elderly—it is the most common psychological disorder of late life, affecting at least five million people sixty-five and older. Yet in this population the problem is very often ignored or overlooked, and it is frequently confused with other physical ailments.

This chapter explains why depression in the elderly is so often overlooked. It gives you guidelines to help you know when your parents are most at risk for depression, and it helps you talk to them about this disease, one they may be embarrassed or ashamed to talk about.

WHY TALK ABOUT DEPRESSION

"I think you're depressed," Mark firmly told his dad. "You never want to come over for dinner anymore. You seem to have no interest in your grandchildren. You just mope around this big, old house by yourself day after day. I'll bet you can't even remember the last time you smiled!" Mark's dad turned away and abruptly dismissed the idea. "You and your fancy psychological diagnosis," he yelled at his son. "A man wants a little peace and quiet by himself and doesn't run around doing a jig, and you decide he's depressed. Maybe you think I should go to one of those shrinks and we can talk about my childhood and my parents and that will make me feel better! Is that what you want?"

As Mark found out, it's not easy to talk to the elderly about depression because they often don't have all the facts about this disease. They are from a generation that still holds firmly to these common myths:

- Depression is not a disease; it is an emotional condition caused by personal weakness.
- Depressed people cry all day.
- There is no cure for depression other than a strong will to "get over it."
- Depression is to be expected in the elderly.

All these myths give you good reasons to talk to your parents about depression if you suspect they are at risk. You can give them the facts that make it easier for them to seek help. Among the many good reasons to talk to your parents about depression, you'll find these at the top of the list:

- Depression is a treatable disease. More than 80 percent of people who receive treatment experience a significant improvement.
- Depression is much more than a feeling of sadness. The symptoms can also include nervousness, anxiety, sleep problems, loss of appetite, and physical aches and pains without identifiable cause.
- Depression is not part of normal aging.
- Depression can be more isolating and socially debilitating than any other chronic illness.

- Depression can be deadly. The rate of suicide among people over eighty is up to six times the rate of suicide in teenagers or young adults.
- Depression negatively affects all members of the family. The sadness, irritability, nervousness, and anxiety associated with depression can be contagious. Other members of the family often find it very difficult to live with a depressed person and soon lose patience and compassion.
- If not treated, depression can have a profound effect on the physical health of an elderly person by exacerbating all other medical illnesses. It can increase cognitive impairment and intensify pain and other medical symptoms. It can also cause a person to neglect necessary medical care.
- Depression often goes undiagnosed because its symptoms are similar to other medical conditions common in the elderly. Alzheimer's disease, Parkinson's disease, and mini-strokes, for example, can cause symptoms that mimic depression, such as lethargy, sleep impairment, difficulty concentrating, self-pity, brooding, pessimism, and loss of appetite.

All these reasons boil down to one underlying fact: unless you talk about the disease of depression to your parents when you see they are at risk, the problem is unlikely to be diagnosed and treated, and the consequences of this neglect can be severe.

WHEN TO TALK ABOUT DEPRESSION

Gail saw the signs but didn't put it all together until it was too late. She knew that her seventy-year-old father had never recovered emotionally from the death of her mother ten years earlier. And she watched with heavy heart as each year he became more withdrawn and more difficult to talk to. She encouraged him to see a doctor when it became obvious that he was losing weight. And she tried to get her dad out of the house and keep him involved in family activities, but even when he agreed to have a holiday meal with her, he was quiet and sullen. "At first," remembers Gail, "it was kind of cute the way he missed my mother. And then I guess I just accepted his sadness as normal. But I had no idea how much pain he was in and how much he needed medical help." Gail's father eventually committed suicide by closing the garage doors and sitting in his car with the engine running. Although Gail isn't to blame for this sad ending, she does live with regrets. "I wish I had paid more attention to his symptoms and helped him talk about his feelings," she says sadly. "Maybe it would have made a difference."

Just as there is no reason to sit down and have a serious conversation with your parents about cancer if you have no reason to suspect they are at risk for the disease, there is no reason to delve into the facts about depression unless you have a reason for concern, as Gail did. This section explains why you should talk about the possibility of depression when

- You suspect your parent is at risk
- Your parent is suffering through a time of loss
- You see the telltale signs and symptoms of depression

When You Suspect Your Parent Is at Risk
You should be on the lookout for signs of depression if your parent has any of these risk factors commonly associated with depression:

- Being female (According to the *Diagnostic and Statistical Manual of Mental Disorders*, a woman's lifetime risk for major depression ranges from 10 to 25 percent, compared with 5 to 12 percent for men.)

- Having a personal family history of depression (A person with one depressed parent has a 26 percent higher risk of depression; one with two depressed parents carries a 46 percent higher risk.)
- Having a chronic illness or caring for someone who does

When Your Parent Is Suffering Through a Time of Loss

Aging often brings with it a sense of great loss—loss of youth, loss of career, loss of independence, loss of good health, and so on. These losses create fertile ground for depression. You should be aware of your parent's feelings during these times of loss and be attentive to signs of depression. Also be aware that these losses shouldn't be used as an excuse for ignoring depression. Saying "Moving into the nursing home has been very difficult for Dad. It's understandable that he is depressed" and then doing nothing about it is like saying "His blood sugar is very high, so it's understandable that he has diabetes" and doing nothing about it. Both are medical illnesses that can and should be treated.

- Loss of Good Health. Forgetfulness, painful joints, bad teeth, cataracts—these and other ailments afflict many elderly people. If seen as signs of "getting old," they can cause great remorse—and eventually lead to depression. Also, major health problems can cause pain, isolation, and inactivity, possibly triggering a depressive episode that will be overlooked because the medical focus is placed on the initial medical problem.

- Loss of independence. As your parent relies more on others (you, neighbors, health care professionals) for help with her daily activities, she may mourn the loss of her independence. If she moves to some sort of senior housing, she may also mourn the loss of her privacy and independence. Depression among the nursing home population is estimated to be as high as 20 to 30 percent.

• Loss of loved ones. As your parent ages, so do his spouse, siblings, and good friends. Each death is a great loss and a reminder of his own mortality. Although grief is normal, extended grief can set off emotional and biochemical changes that can lead to depression. About 20 percent of the 800,000 newly widowed Americans become depressed each year for about two months after the loss. About one-third of them stay depressed for up to one year.

• Loss of companionship. Your parent's life used to be busy, even hectic. Family, work, and friends all vied for attention. In later life, however, things slow down after the children move out, the retirement party is over, and old friends move away. There is a great sense of loss in loneliness.

When You See the Telltale Signs and Symptoms of Depression

A doctor makes a diagnosis of major depression based on certain standard criteria outlined in the *Diagnostic and Statistical Manual of Mental Disorders (DSM IV)*. According to this manual, you should suspect depression if you see at least five of the following symptoms persist nearly every day for at least two weeks and if these symptoms represent a change from the way the individual has felt or functioned in the past:

1. Depressed mood (feeling sad or empty or seeming sad or tearful)
2. Greatly diminished interest or pleasure in all or almost all activities

3. Significant weight gain or loss without dieting, or increased or decreased appetite
4. Sleeping much more or much less than usual
5. Observable slowing down or speeding up of activity
6. Fatigue or loss of energy
7. Feelings of worthlessness or excessive or inappropriate guilt
8. Diminished ability to think or concentrate, or indecisiveness
9. Recurrent thoughts of death (not just fear of dying), recurrent suicidal thoughts without a specific plan, or a suicide attempt or specific plan for committing suicide

These signs and symptoms give you reason to talk to your parent about the possibility of depression, but don't jump on this diagnosis without professional medical help. These same signs and symptoms can be the result of physical illness (such as hypothyroidism, diabetes, and heart disease) or abuse of alcohol or drugs.

Many of these symptoms can be caused by the medications your parent may be taking. Many medications that slow down the body systems or change body chemistry can cause depression. And in other cases, medications can cause reactions that mimic the symptoms of depression. Medications associated with depressive symptoms include some anticonvulsants, antihistamines, antihypertensives and other cardiac drugs, anti-Parkinson's agents, benzodiazepines (used to treat anxiety), corticosteroids (used to treat arthritis, asthma, and cancer, among other conditions), and hormones. Changing the medication or even the dosage can offer a quick remedy.

When you suspect that your parent is suffering depression, it's time for a talk about getting a thorough medical checkup that includes a psychological evaluation.

WHAT YOU SHOULD TALK ABOUT

Talking to elderly parents about the signs of depression is sensitive business. Depending on your relationship and the kind of communication you have established over the years, you may or may not get your parent to open up and talk about her feelings and ask for help. But at the very least, you can talk to her about your own observations, concerns, and desire to help.

Breaking the Ice

When you decide to talk to your parent about the possibility of depression, remember that the word *depression* has a stigma attached for many of the older generation. It is something that crazy people get. It is not something that strong, independent people get. Many elderly people grew up in a time when feeling "sad" was seen as a moral failing, and they tend to harbor a strong sense that if they would only pull themselves up by the bootstraps they could overcome this.

If you sense this resistance to the idea of depression, use the word sparingly, and instead talk about the symptoms. Rather than say, "You seem depressed to me," you might say, "You seem very sad, and I've noticed that you don't go out very often any more. Why is that?" It's a simple change in word choice that can make a big difference in the way your parent will react to your concern.

Whatever the circumstance in your family or the details of the parent's depression, keep these tips in mind when you have conversations about this subject:

- Be compassionate
- Be accepting
- Be empathic

- Be patient
- Choose your words carefully

Be Compassionate.   In theory, of course, you will speak compassionately with a person who is depressed. In practice it is much harder. A depressed parent may not return your phone calls, may grunt one-syllable answers or talk for hours about pain and problems, may have no interest in doing anything, may act completely self-absorbed. This is a recipe for anger rather than compassion, but it's important to keep calm. Remind yourself that your parent has a disease and that her actions are not totally voluntary. Even though your efforts may not appear to be appreciated, experts say that social support during times of depression is very important.

Be Accepting.   It's natural to try to cheer up a depressed person. But when you point out all the good things in life and try to convince a depressed person that he really has nothing to be sad about, you tend to trivialize those deep feelings and push the person further away. Instead, listen and accept your parent's emotions and perceptions as real.

Be Empathic.   Don't argue when your parent says something that sounds ridiculous to you, such as "I have nothing to live for. Nobody cares about me." Instead, you might say that you understand how hopeless and disappointing life can be at times. Help her express these feelings of despair without being judgmental.

Be Patient.   Depression is a process that takes time to develop, time to cause alarm, time to understand, and time to resolve. Let your parent know that you offer your support no matter how long it takes and that you will always be there when he wants to talk.

Choose Your Words Carefully. When you talk to your parent about depression, keep these communication tips in mind:

Instead of saying: "It can't be that bad. You have had such a good life. What are you so sad about?"
You might say: "I know you haven't been feeling well lately, and I care about what's happening to you. How about we go out for lunch on Saturday?"

Instead of saying: "Don't dwell on your problems so much."
You might say: "I'm just calling to say hello and tell you I love you."

Instead of saying: "There's nothing wrong with you. Cheer up."
You might say: "I don't know exactly what you're feeling, but I'm here for you."

Instead of saying: "Instead of complaining all the time, why don't you do something to help yourself?"
You might say: "I can see that you're unhappy. Let's think of something we can do to help you get better."

Instead of saying: "Stop crying. I thought you were stronger than that."
You might say: "Don't be afraid. I'll help you."

Addressing Specific Issues

The details of a conversation about depression will depend on your parent's willingness to talk about her feelings and physical symptoms. This section offers some conversation starters on the following topics related to depression:

- The facts
- The difference between depression and sadness
- The symptoms of depression

- Signs of substance abuse
- Thoughts of suicide
- Treatment options

Talk About the Facts.   Depression is a physical disease caused by an imbalance of the brain chemicals responsible for transmitting messages about mood and behavior. When these chemicals no longer function effectively, depression may be the result. Studies have found that aging can cause a change in the production of these chemicals, which can predispose some elderly to depression even when there is no "sad" event to trigger feelings of loss or emptiness. Your parent needs to know that depression has a physical cause that can be treated.

You might say: "Dad, you don't seem to be yourself anymore. I've noticed that you haven't been keeping up the house, and you've mentioned that you've gotten behind on your bills. I'm wondering if maybe you should talk to your doctor about these things. I've read that several medical conditions like anemia and thyroid disease can affect a person's energy level and make it difficult to do daily activities. I've also read that as we age there is often a change in the production of certain brain chemicals, which can cause depression and affect the way we feel and act. The right prescription medication can correct these imbalances. Maybe you should talk to your doctor about this. What do you think?" (Remember, if you know your parent will resist the idea of "depression," you can couch the facts about this disease by referring to it as a medical condition—which it is.)

Talk About the Difference Between Depression and Sadness.
We all go through periods of feeling sad and frustrated with life experiences, but depression is different. Sadness is usually attached

to a specific life event, such as the loss of a loved one or a financial failure. But depression often does not have a clear cause; even if there is a cause, depression persists long after the triggering event has passed.

It can be very difficult to distinguish sadness from depression—the symptoms of normal grief are not entirely different from those of depression (see the preceding chapter, "Grief and Bereavement"); it is a matter of degree. Although normal grief can cause changes in appetite, sleeping habits, and other behavior, depression may show itself in extremes of behavior: not eating or eating too much, not sleeping or sleeping too much, complete withdrawal or talking incessantly, being extremely hostile or totally apathetic. If these extremes continue for a prolonged time (more than two weeks), it's time to talk about depression and what to do about it.

Your parents need to know that it is normal to sometimes feel sad but that it is not normal to be depressed. Without treatment, this illness is likely to get worse.

You might say: "I know it's normal to feel sad occasionally, but I'm worried that your feelings of sadness are lasting such a long time. And I've also noticed that you haven't been eating much lately and don't go out with your friends very often. There's a difference between being sad and having a medial problem that can make you feel this way. Why don't you call your doctor for a checkup this week?"

Talk About the Symptoms of Depression. It's not "normal" for the elderly to be depressed. Talk to your parent if you see any of these typical signs of depression:

Unexplained Changes in Emotional Health. These include feelings of

- Emptiness. Your parent may feel hollow inside—not sad, not angry, not happy—just empty.
- Hopelessness. Your parent may feel that nothing good is going to happen in the future. "It doesn't matter; I won't be around much longer anyway."
- Remorse. Your parent may get stuck in the past where things should have been different and life could have been better.
- Guilt. Depression causes fatigue and listlessness. Things don't get done. Promises are broken. Appointments are canceled. When these things happen, some people feel a strong sense of guilt that translates into "I'm no good. I don't deserve such a loving family. I always let everybody down."

You might say: "I've noticed that you don't seem to be enjoying life as you used to, and I wanted to talk to you about that. What do you think about the way you've been feeling lately?"

Unexplained Changes in Physical Health.   Emotional changes are an important clue to the onset of depression, but they are not the only symptoms. In fact, physical changes related to depression may occur before the emotional ones. Watch for unexplained pain, headaches, decreased energy, stomach problems, insomnia or hypersomnia, loss or increase in appetite.

You might say: "I'm worried about you. You've been complaining of so many medical problems that just won't go away. Have you thought about making an appointment with your doctor?"

Unexplained Changes in Cognitive Health.   Depression often causes mental cloudiness and confusion. It can show itself as memory loss, language inhibition, difficulty with concentration, diminished learning capacity, and even delusions and hallucinations.

Unfortunately, these symptoms are usually ignored in the elderly as "normal." As explained in the chapter on dementia, mental confusion is not normal at any age and should be brought to a doctor's attention. If your parent is suffering Alzheimer's disease, this symptom of depression is easily overlooked as "expected"; and sometimes depression is misdiagnosed as Alzheimer's, causing much unnecessary heartache.

Look for these differences to distinguish dementia from depression: in Alzheimer's and most other forms of dementia, recent memory becomes seriously impaired, but early-life memories remain much longer. In depression, early memories are usually affected as well. Also, antidepressant medication will not affect the cognitive problems of dementia but will usually relieve the cognitive symptoms of depression.

You might say: "I know you're concerned about problems with forgetfulness and memory. Have you made an appointment with your doctor? These symptoms can be early symptoms of things like Alzheimer's, but they can also be caused by other medical conditions that can be easily treated."

Unexplained Behavioral Changes.   Depression affects not only how a person feels but also how he acts. Depressed people may withdraw from socializing. They often lose interest in things they previously loved. They may become irritable and cranky. They may complain about physical ailments that have no observable cause.

You might say: "Mom, you used to enjoy visiting with your grandchildren, and you don't anymore. It seems like you feel annoyed when you are around them. We're all worried about that. I'm wondering if there might be something physically wrong going on that you should get checked out. Would you call your doctor this week and set up a medical exam and some blood tests?"

Watch for Signs of Substance Abuse. Alcohol and drug abuse can be tightly woven into the problem of depression in the elderly, often either masking the symptoms of depression or causing them. People who are vulnerable to depression may use alcohol or medication to alter their mood. Consciously or unconsciously they may use alcohol or drugs to self-medicate the symptoms of depression. Unfortunately, the physical, social, and psychological problems associated with substance abuse give them more reason to be depressed, thus bringing them further down into the hold of hopelessness, isolation, and sadness. They then feel the need to use more alcohol or medication to pull themselves back up. It's a vicious cycle. If your parent may be abusing alcohol or medication, be sure to read the chapter "Late-Onset Alcoholism," and be aware of the possibility that this abuse is connected to underlying depression.

Talk About Thoughts of Suicide. Left untreated, depression can put the elderly at serious risk for suicide. Compared with all other age groups, seniors commit suicide twice as frequently. Suicides are especially common among elderly men, who account for 81 percent of suicides of those over sixty-five. The National Institutes of Mental Health report a particularly tragic situation: 70 percent of elderly people who commit suicide visit their family doctors within a month before their death, and 39 percent have a medical encounter within one week of killing themselves, yet their depression remains undiagnosed and untreated.

Given these frightening statistics, you should not be afraid to talk to your parent about suicide if he has been dropping hints like,

"I'm no use to anyone. I'd be better off dead." Bringing up the subject will not cause your parent to become suicidal or push him to
carry out his threats. Talking about this subject shows you take his
feelings seriously. However, don't give a lecture on the value of life
to remind your parent of all the good things worth living for. Of
course there is a tendency to say, "These should be the best years of
your life. Why are you feeling so sad?" But when you lecture like this
you imply very strongly that a person has total control over depression, and that is not the case. Depression is a biological illness much
like diabetes, heart disease, or stroke. Although there are ways we
can improve mood, we cannot control the course of depression just
by willing it away. If you remind your parent that he should be
happy, he will feel a greater sense of shame and failure than he is
already feeling.

If you suspect your parent is suicidal, don't get emotional and
excited. Try to be very matter-of-fact. If you are comfortable talking
to your parent about this subject, you might say, "It is not at all
unusual for people who feel depressed to think about trying to escape
the pain through suicide. Have you ever thought about that?"

It is usually difficult for a son or daughter to discuss suicide
with a parent who is supposed to be the one in control. So it is
more common to enlist the help of a professional, such as the family practitioner, a psychiatrist, or someone at a crisis clinic hotline.
If the parent absolutely refuses help, as a last resort you may need
to bring a mental health professional into the home to do an evaluation and determine if your parent should be forced to be admitted to the hospital.

Talk About Treatment Options.   Mild depression may respond well
to at-home therapies. Support from family and friends, opportunities

for social activities, exercise, and long talks often help individuals with otherwise good coping skills. But in many cases, depression does not respond to self-help remedies. In these cases, a thorough physical and mental medical evaluation is necessary. Usually the best place to start an evaluation of depression is with the primary health care provider. Your parent is probably comfortable with this person and is more likely to make an appointment and talk freely about her symptoms than she would be if you were to arrange a psychiatric evaluation with a psychiatrist or psychologist right off the bat (although a referral to one of these specialists may come later).

It's usually not best for you to take charge and make the appointment for your parent. Unless there is reason to suspect the possibility of suicide or some form of dementia, it is better to form a partnership with your parent that allows you to help and guide her and that at the same time maintains her dignity and independence.

You might say: "What do you think? Do you want to see your doctor about these symptoms? Would you like me to give him a call?"

Because the symptoms of depression in the elderly can be masked by other illness, by medication, and by the elderly person's resistance to talking openly about feelings, depression is often missed at a routine checkup. For this reason, if your parent agrees to get a medical checkup, it would be appropriate for you to call ahead and explain to the doctor that you would like her to consider the possibility of depression as part of her examination. Doing so is important because it alerts the doctor to the need to schedule some extra time to talk about these symptoms of concern.

Although the physician will explain the treatment options if depression is diagnosed, before meeting with the doctor your parent may be worried about what will happen to him. If this is the case, you can explain that there are generally three treatment options:

1. Medication. Medications for depression alter the action of brain chemicals so as to improve mood, sleep, appetite, energy levels, and concentration.
2. Psychotherapy. Talking with a trained therapist can effectively treat some types of depression. Short-term therapies (usually twelve to twenty sessions) focus on the specific symptoms of depression. Cognitive therapy aims to help the individual recognize and change negative thinking patterns that contribute to depression. Interpersonal therapy focuses on dealing more effectively with other people in the belief that improving relationships can sometimes reduce depressive symptoms.
3. Biological treatments. Electroconvulsive therapy is an effective treatment that is used in cases of extreme depression. This is an option a mental health professional may recommend when rapid improvement is necessary (to prevent suicide, for example) or when medications have failed. During treatment, anesthesia and muscle relaxant medication protect the person from pain or physical harm. Improved procedures make this treatment much safer than in previous years, when the idea of "shock therapy" was very frightening.

Talking to your parent about his struggle with depression is a great gift of love, but you have to accept your own limitations when you do this. You cannot free your parent of this disease by yourself, nor can you be responsible for how he chooses to treat it. But by keeping a dialogue going that focuses on your parent's feelings and needs, you may find that you create a stronger and more empathic relationship that will benefit both of you.

RESOURCES

American Psychiatric Association
1400 K Street NW
Washington, DC 20005
(202) 682-6220
www.psych.org

American Psychological Association
750 First Street NE
Washington, DC 20002
(202) 336-5500
www.apa.org

National Alliance for the Mentally Ill
2101 Wilson Boulevard, Suite 302
Arlington, VA 22201
(703) 524-7600
www.naimi.org

National Foundation for Depressive Illness
P.O. Box 2257
New York, NY 10016
(212) 268-4260
www.depression.org

National Institutes of Mental Health
Bethesda, MD
Public inquiries: (301) 443-4513
www.nimh.nih.gov (website)
nimhinfo@nih.gov (e-mail)

National Mental Health Association
1021 Prince Street
Alexandria, VA 23314
(800) 969-6642
www.nmha.org

EXPERT HELP

This chapter was written with the expert help of Patrick Mathiasen, M.D., a psychiatrist who is board certified in both adult psychiatry and geriatric psychiatry. Dr. Mathiasen is the former medical director of the geriatric psychiatry unit at Northwest Hospital in Seattle, Washington. He is a clinical assistant professor at the University of Washington and the author of the books *Late Life Depression* (Dell, 1997) and *An Ocean of Time, Alzheimer's: Tales of Hope and Forgetting* (Scribner, 1997).

Dementia

Knowing how to talk to an elderly parent with dementia can open doors to a wonderful relationship and replace conflict with loving interaction.

> Janice Knebl, DO, *chief of geriatrics at the University of North Texas Health Science Center*

At first Gary simply thought his father was not as mentally sharp as he used to be; after all, the man was eighty-two years old—he shouldn't be expected to remember everything. Gary figured, what harm was there if his father called him twice a day to tell him the same story over again? But then he noticed other cognitive problems. Gary's dad began to forget to pay his bills, and the letters from collection agencies were piling up. He was not as well groomed as usual; he was frequently unshaven, and his clothes often looked soiled. He couldn't remember names or phone numbers. He had trouble making rather simple decisions. And last week he asked Gary if he knew when his mother would be coming home, even though he knows she died ten years ago. What was Gary supposed to say to a question like that?

125

W ithout a doubt it is very difficult to talk to elderly parents about the subject of dementia—but it can and should be done, as this subject of conversation becomes more and more common each day. The U.S. Congress Office of Technology Assessment estimates that 1.8 million Americans have severe dementia and another 1 to 5 million Americans have mild to moderate dementia. According to the Alzheimer's Association, approximately 4 million of these people are afflicted with Alzheimer's disease. By the year 2040, the number of persons with Alzheimer's disease may exceed 6 million. Dementia will affect many of our parents—but what will we say?

This chapter explores the many times and ways you can talk to your parents about failing mental skills. It also helps you know how to talk to a parent whose cognitive skills are declining, and it gives you the words you need when your aging parent asks you when your deceased mother will be home.

WHY TALK ABOUT DEMENTIA

Dementia is a loose term used to describe someone with significant memory loss and impairment in cognitive function. Your parents may use the word *senility* to describe the same condition. In the past, senility was chalked off as an unavoidable consequence of aging, and there was nothing to do or say when Mom or Dad began to show signs of slipping. But experts today say that no one develops dementia as part of normal aging; it happens when the parts of the brain that are involved with learning, memory, decision making, and language are affected by any of various neurological, vascular, infectious, or metabolic diseases—but not because the brain gets old. In fact, some types of dementia are treatable, and others can be quite successfully treated if caught early.

This fact gives you a strong reason to talk to your parents about dementia—its diagnosis and treatment—before it's too late. As your parents become more and more forgetful, they may be terrified that a trip to the doctor will confirm their fear of Alzheimer's disease. They need to know that there are many causes of dementia, including strokes, low vitamin B-12 levels, thyroid conditions, depression, AIDS, and viral and fungal infections of the brain. Medications, some illnesses, and substance abuse can cause confusion (delirium) in older people that may look like dementia. Such metabolic disorders as thyroid problems, nutritional deficiencies, and anemias also can mimic symptoms of dementia. Neurological and circulatory disorders as well as injuries to the head, any type of tumor within the skull, and even carbon monoxide poisoning can cause symptoms that can be confused with dementia. All these conditions can be treated if caught early enough—if you talk to your parents about their symptoms and make sure they get good medical care.

In order to give our elderly parents extra years of mental sharpness, we need to shake off the fatalistic belief that forgetfulness is natural and that nothing can be done for it. When James noticed that his mother was forgetful, he didn't turn his back on the situation. He sat right down and asked her if she had noticed that she was having trouble remembering things. He asked her about her last medical checkup. He asked her to make another appointment to discuss with her doctor her own concerns about her mental health. "After all," he encouraged her, "you have a lot of living yet to do, and I want you to be in the best of physical and mental health for as long as possible. I know you're not ready to have me beat you at a game of bridge just yet." Part of keeping our parents mentally healthy involves being willing to talk about the subject of dementia—that's why you shouldn't hesitate to put this subject on the table.

WHEN TO TALK ABOUT DEMENTIA

As is the case with many subjects, the best time to talk about dementia is before it is a problem. This is a subject that you might begin talking about when you have a family member or friend who is suffering from advanced stages of the disease or when some notable person suffering Alzheimer's disease is in the news. These situations give you a good opportunity to have a general discussion about the fine line between normal forgetfulness (forgetting where your keys are) and early signs of dementia (forgetting which car is yours in the parking lot).

You should begin talking about a medical evaluation when you see the signs discussed in this section:

- Short-term memory loss
- Psychiatric symptoms

When There Is Short-Term Memory Loss

The first symptoms in a disease like Alzheimer's involve short-term memory loss. Helen began to notice these signs in her mother, Rose—occasional and minor at first and then more frequent and serious. Rose often had trouble finding the words she needed to tell a story; last week, she was talking about the gift she had bought for her best friend, but couldn't remember the friend's name. She would forget where she had put the bag of groceries, the mail, or her shoes; she had started to ask Helen to come over and help her look for these kinds of everyday items. Rose would also forget appointments;

recently she completely forgot that Helen was going to pick her up to go shopping even though they had made the arrangements just a few hours earlier.

The following are classic signs of early dementia. Don't ignore them; they indicate it's time for a talk.

- Repeating things
- Having trouble finding or speaking the right word
- Forgetting to turn off the stove, close windows, or lock doors
- Forgetting appointments
- Getting lost while driving
- Having trouble keeping track of money

These symptoms appear gradually in persons with Alzheimer's disease, but may progress more slowly in some than in others. In other forms of dementia, symptoms may appear suddenly or may come and go.

When There Are Psychiatric Symptoms

Signs of dementia can also appear as psychiatric problems. Memory problems make some people appear agitated and worried. You may see mood and personality changes as well. Some people eventually become paranoid. This was the case with Sam's dad. "Last month I was shocked when he accused me of taking money from his wallet," Sam remembers. "He knows I would never do that, but he kept insisting. I think he didn't know what had happened to that money, so rather than face the possibility that his memory was failing, he decided to blame me." Sam noticed that his dad also was becoming very withdrawn and angry; he rarely came out to his grandkids' ball games anymore, and when he did visit for dinner, he seemed very demanding and difficult to please. "I don't know what's got into him lately, but he's really tough to be around," says Sam. "He's pushed us all away, and now he spends his days alone and bitter. Is that what he wants?"

It's most likely that Sam's dad hasn't consciously separated himself from his family, and he certainly doesn't want to be left alone. An elderly person can exhibit these kinds of behaviors when he is running scared or when his behavior is suddenly out of his control due to progressive dementia.

You'll know it's time to talk to your parent about her mental health when she begins to

- Accuse others of taking things from her (because she can't remember where she put these things)
- Become withdrawn (because she fears others will notice she's "going senile")
- Become demanding and bossy (because she's afraid or is suffering memory loss)

If your parent is behaving differently than what you would call normal, this is a sign that you should talk to her about having a medical evaluation.

WHAT YOU SHOULD TALK ABOUT

Conversations about dementia change over time as the problem progresses. At first, it's a good idea to talk in general terms to break the ice on this sensitive subject. Then it's time to be more specific and talk about situations that pertain to your parent's needs and weaknesses.

What to Say About Possible Dementia

In the following sections, you'll find information that will help you know what to say if you suspect dementia, and you'll also find the words to talk to a parent who is in the later stages of mental confusion.

Because dementia is part of your parent's entire health picture, you do not have to talk immediately about his memory problems when you first notice them. If you are concerned about upsetting him, talk about his health in general at first. Everyone over the age of sixty-five should have a thorough medical checkup at least once a year. Instead of focusing on his mental health only, you can tell him that you are concerned about his health and want him to get a medical checkup.

When your parent has a medical appointment, it would be appropriate for you to call the physician and mention your concern about cognitive function. You could also offer to go with your parent to the doctor's appointment. The more information a physician has at hand during the exam and evaluation, the more accurate the diagnosis he or she can make.

If, after your parent gets a clean bill of health, he gets upset because he forgets where he put his keys and worries that this is a sign of Alzheimer's, you can remind him that he often lost his keys forty years ago as well. If you see no other signs of dementia, you might clarify for your parent the difference between age-associated memory loss and dementia. Those with age-associated memory loss may take longer to remember things than they used to, but they can eventually retrieve the information. They may not be able to come up with their granddaughter's name immediately when they want it, but in a few moments it will come to them. This is perfectly normal. But those with dementia, which is a disease, cannot come up with the information they want. Not only may they be unable to ever recall their granddaughter's name, but they may not remember they have a granddaughter.

You might say: "I'm sure there's nothing wrong with your mind right now; everyone forgets things once in awhile."

But don't lose this opportunity to talk about the subject of dementia.

You might say: "But if years from now I notice that you do seem to be having difficulty with your memory, would you want me to talk to you about it? What would you like me to do for you?"

If your parent does begin to forget more and more things until one day she forgets your birthday, she will need your reassurance and help. When she begins to cry because she's convinced that her memory problems mean she is on a fast downward spiral into incapacitating dementia, it's not helpful to offer empty reassurances: "Oh, don't worry. You'll be just fine. There's nothing wrong with you." When surely there is something wrong, this kind of response is a form a denial that hurts both of you. But it's also not necessary to scare your parent.

Instead of saying: "You need to see a doctor about your memory problem."
You might say: "There are lots of reasons someone can have memory problems. Depression and some medications, for example, are known to cause memory problems. Because you're concerned about your health, why don't you make an appointment to see your doctor and talk about it."

If a forgetful parent comes to you and asks, "Do you think my memory is slipping?" you probably won't have the medical knowledge you need to make an on-the-spot diagnosis of dementia. But you might help your parent decide for himself if he should seek medical treatment by showing him the following list of questions that the National Library of Medicine at the National Institutes of Health offers to help the elderly decide if they have early signs of dementia.

- Learning and remembering new information
  Do you repeat things that you say or do?
  Do you forget conversations or appointments? Forget where you put things?
- Handling complex tasks
  Do you have trouble performing tasks that require many steps, such as balancing a checkbook or cooking a meal?
- Reasoning ability
  Do you have trouble solving everyday problems at work or home, such as knowing what to do if the bathroom is flooded?
- Spatial ability and orientation
  Do you have trouble driving or finding your way around familiar places?
- Language
  Do you have trouble finding the words to express what you want to say?
- Behavior
  Do you have trouble paying attention?
  Are you more irritable or less trusting than usual?

If your parent answers yes to a number of these questions but resists getting medical attention because she assumes there is nothing anyone can do to help her, talk about the constructive things that can come from good medical care.

You might say: "There are a number of reasons to get a good medical evaluation. First, there are other causes of dementia and confusion that can be very easily treated. People with confusion may return to normal once the medications are changed or the illness is treated. Second, if it should happen that you do have Alzheimer's disease, there are now new treatments that seem to improve the symptoms and slow the progression of the disease. Third, the doctor will be able to refer you to community resources for information, support groups, and other help at home."

What to Say When Your Parent Has Dementia

Even with the best medical care, cases of true dementia will eventually progress and affect your parent's memory, problem-solving ability, decision making, judgment, and ability to put together simple sentences and understand and communicate with words. If this has happened to your parent, you'll need to rethink how you talk to him.

It's important to understand that correcting your parent's mistakes will not affect her ability to remember. You can remind your mother twenty-four hours a day that you are her second child, Nancy, and not her first child, Gloria, and you still will not make her remember that. You will find it much easier to talk with your parent in this condition if you go where she is mentally rather than insist that she come into your reality. This is not easy at first, but if you can let yourself relax and accept your parent's view of her world, you can have wonderful conversations rather than arguments.

If, for example, your mother looks up at the blue summer sky and says what a bright purple sky it is, it's not necessary to correct her and insist that the sky is blue. You're not going to convince her it's blue, and you have to ask yourself if it's really worth arguing over. Instead, go with her and enjoy the purple sky. Comment on what an unusual shade of purple it is. Ask her if purple is a color she likes. Go off on a conversation about this color. That's where your mother is at that moment; it's easier for both of you if you go there.

You also can learn to enjoy conversations with your parent if you let go of your resistance to his focus on the past. Yes, it gets tiring to hear the same stories of Uncle Bob and his harmonica over and over again, but when the short-term memory goes, this may be all your parent has left to hang on to. Rather than try to make your parent talk about today and tomorrow (which are places he may not have the ability to mentally imagine), join him in his strolls down memory lane and ask him questions. It's likely that you'll learn things you never knew about your parent.

This focus on the past can be uncomfortable for you at first if your parent talks about deceased family members as though they were still alive. Again, don't try to get your parent to accept the "truth." If your dad wonders aloud if your mom will be home for dinner, you don't need to insist, "Dad, you know Mom died five years ago." Instead, go where he is. Enjoy a little reminiscing. Ask him what Mom liked to cook for dinner. It's as easy as that—yet it's so hard.

When you talk to your parent as her ability to articulate her thoughts and feelings diminishes, you'll need to change your own style of communicating. Keep these tips in mind when you sit down to talk to your parent:

- Speak slowly and calmly.
- Use short, simple, direct sentences.
- Discuss only one subject at a time. You can spend the whole afternoon talking about the flowers in the garden.
- Ask simple questions that are not open ended. Rather than ask, "What did you have for dinner?" ask, "What vegetables did you eat at dinner?"

- Don't hesitate to repeat information if your parent seems confused and unable to follow the story line.
- Treat your parent like an adult, not a child.

Every conversation you have with your elderly parent helps him maintain memory, improve listening skills, and practice the art of conversation. At any stage of dementia, talking is a real skill builder.

RESOURCES

Alzheimer's Association
919 North Michigan Avenue, Suite 1000
Chicago, IL 60611
(800) 272-3900

This nonprofit group supports families and caregivers of Alzheimer's patients. Chapters nationwide provide referrals to local resources and services, and sponsor support groups and educational programs.

Alzheimer's Disease Education and Referral (ADEAR) Center
P.O. Box 8250
Silver Spring, MD 20907
(800) 438-4380
adear@alzheimers.org (e-mail)

This service of the National Institute on Aging is funded by the federal government. It offers information and publications on diagnosis, treatment, patient care, caregiver needs, long-term care, education and training, and research related to Alzheimer's. Staff respond to telephone and written requests and make referrals to national and state-level resources.

National Alzheimer's Association
(800) 272-3900
www.alz.org

This organization is the largest national voluntary health organization dedicated to funding research into the causes, treatments, prevention, and cure of Alzheimer's disease and to providing support to the four million Americans with the disease, their families, and caregivers. It has a network of chapters across the country. Support groups and helplines provided by this network help people live and cope with Alzheimer's disease. The Alzheimer's Association also provides informational materials, including brochures, fact sheets, and checklists to help families learn about Alzheimer's disease and important topics, including caregiving strategies and legal and financial issues.

EXPERT HELP

This chapter was written with the expert help of Janice Knebl, DO, CMD, FACP, FACOI, chief of geriatrics at the University of North Texas Health Science Center at Fort Worth, Texas. She has been trained in Alzheimer's and dementia care and serves as the medical director of the Heritage Geriatric Centers of Excellence, specifically for Alzheimer's residents, and as the medical codirector of the James L. West Special Care Dementia Center.

Part Three

Housing

Choosing to Live at Home

The main reason to have a conversation about home care is to assure an elderly person that he or she can stay at home as long as possible and still have the support necessary to do this safely.

Angela Heath, National Association
of Area Agencies on Aging

The family holiday gathering was just perfect. Katlyn and her two brothers, along with all their spouses and children, got together to celebrate Thanksgiving in the home Katlyn and her brothers had grown up in. Although well into her seventies, Katlyn's mother was proud to be living on her own and to have a place where her children and her grandchildren could come together. Times like this convinced Katlyn's mother that she would never leave her home—never.

Katlyn understood her mother's feelings, but still she worried about this decision. Keeping the house cleaned and maintained was a big job. And if she stayed alone, how could anyone know if she was eating properly? And taking her medications? And getting out to socialize? How long could she realistically keep doing this?

Katlyn's concerns are shared by thousands of adult children every day when their elderly parents make it clear that they do not want to move out of their homes into a more supervised environment, such as an assisted living home or a nursing home. The National Institutes of Health report that only 9 percent of people ages sixty-five through sixty-nine require day-to-day assistance, including help with bathing, dressing, and eating, whereas 50 percent of those age eighty-five and older need this kind of help. They also report that one-third of elderly women age seventy-five and older are functionally dependent and in need of considerable assistance. Given these statistics, if your parents want to stay at home as they age, there's a lot to talk about to make sure they get the services and assistance they need.

This chapter gives you an idea of the kinds of support systems available to elderly people who choose to stay in their own homes. It helps you find the words to talk to your parents about these services and about your willingness to help them stay at home for as long as they can live there safely.

WHY TALK ABOUT LIVING AT HOME

Eighty-two-year-old Jack enjoyed reliving the memories held in each room of the house he had lived in for the last fifty-four years. He could picture as though it were yesterday the vision of his young wife standing over the crib adoring her newborn baby. He could hear the clamoring sounds of the children's footsteps on the stairs and the squeak of the swings in the backyard; he could hear the laughter and songs at the birthday parties through the years. But as he looked around his home now, he was hurt by the obvious signs of neglect.

His prize flowerbeds were overgrown with weeds. The kitchen sink was stained, and the floor was dirty. His own clothes were soiled. He just couldn't keep up any more; his arthritis often bothered him too much to do the chores he used to, and he was just not able to bend over and scrub and clean anymore.

Jack knew his daughter would be disappointed if she ever saw the house looking like this, and she'd be glad to help him straighten things up. But there was no way Jack was going to ask for help. His daughter lived several hours away and visited only a few times a year—the few times Jack pushed himself to get everything in order. "If she knew I couldn't handle this house," he said to himself, "she'd get all crazy about making me move into one of those senior homes." Jack wasn't moving, and he didn't want the bother of arguing with his daughter over that decision, so he put up a good front and assured her every time they spoke that he was just fine living all alone in that big house.

The decision to live at home is often an unspoken one. Your parent simply stays where she is, and life goes on. As she ages, however, your parent may find it more and more difficult to manage on her own, and being isolated in her own home can cause a number of problems that she may be uncomfortable talking to you about. She may fear that if she admits that she no longer cooks for herself or has trouble getting in and out of the tub or is lonely, you'll want to put her in a nursing home. She may be uncomfortable talking to you about personal problems, and she may worry about being a burden. So she remains silent and often unnecessarily puts her physical and emotional health at risk.

If your parent wants to stay in his own home, even when you can clearly see that it is difficult for him to manage on his own, it's time for a talk. Certainly, as long as his health and safety aren't endangered he has a right to live where he chooses—but you can give him the information and resources he may need to help him better manage the activities of daily living.

WHEN TO TALK ABOUT STAYING PUT

Very often the subject of staying at home or moving to a supportive facility comes up for family discussion after some sort of crisis. Tony's mom had lived in the same apartment building all her life. She was born and raised there and then moved into a two-bedroom apartment down the hall from her parents when she married her high school sweetheart. Today Tony's mom is eighty-two; the neighborhood children call her Miss Maisy and knock on her door daily for the cookies she always has ready. But now her son wants her to leave the city and move in with him because the neighborhood has changed over the years and has turned into a high-crime area. In fact, Maisy's apartment was recently burglarized. Fortunately Maisy wasn't home at the time, but her habit of leaving her door unlocked made her an easy target, and her family is very worried.

If Maisy insists on staying put (as Tony knows she will), he will have a long talk with her about safety. He will install safety locks and an alarm system. He will call her daily to push her into the habit of locking those new locks, and he will ask the neighbors to look in on her each day. He will contact telephone reassurance programs or "friendly visitor" programs. The break-in pushed Tony into action; his mother is now more secure than she had been, and this is a good thing. But it would have been much better if Tony had talked with his mother about her safety before the burglary shook him into action.

Prevention is the topic of conversation that is most useful to your parent when he is living alone in his own home. Talk to him when you see signs of trouble or difficulty. Certainly Tony saw that his mom's neighborhood was becoming a dangerous one. Keep your eyes and ears open so you know when your parent is struggling with his independence. The following are some signs to watch for:

- The home looks neglected or in disrepair.
- There's no food in the refrigerator, or there's old food piling up that may even be spoiled.
- Your parent mentions the difficulty of keeping track of all his medications.
- The lighting in the home is dim, or throw rugs are loose.
- Your parent withdraws and rarely comes out of the house.
- Daily activities (like cooking, washing, laundering, and so on) are clearly difficult for your parent.
- Your parent can no longer drive and seems isolated from friends and necessary services (such as the bank, doctor, and market).
- There is a threat of any kind to your parent's safety.

Knowing when to talk to your parent about her decision to stay in her own home takes some detective work. Keep your eyes open and ask lots of questions.

WHAT YOU SHOULD TALK ABOUT

The details of a conversation about home care will change as your parent ages and his needs change. Karen's dad had a mini-stroke; Karen says, "I live nearby and planned to stop in every day, but I still worried about how he would be able to take care of himself." She sat down to talk with her dad the day he returned home from the hospital. Together they discussed how he would manage living alone. They decided to hire a homemaker who would prepare meals and do light housekeeping. About five months after setting up this arrangement, the homemaker told Karen that her dad passed up an invitation to have lunch with his buddies because he didn't want to "drive through all that traffic"; Karen then sat down with her dad to talk about arranging for transportation whenever he needed it. She also took this opportunity to talk to her dad about what she should do for him if he had another, more serious stroke. He told her that he would like to hire a round-the-clock home health aide rather than move into a nursing home. These conversations and the actions that followed allowed Karen's dad to stay at home far longer than Karen had initially thought possible, and it also gave both of them the peace of mind that comes with knowing what the next step will be.

Breaking the Ice

It can be tough to bring up the subject of "help" when your parent is independent enough to live in her own home. It's a good idea to break the ice on this subject before you suggest something like bringing a "stranger" into her home to help her live safely. You can break the ice and reduce misunderstandings if you talk about

- Your own difficulties managing your home
- Other elderly people who manage their own homes
- Gift certificates for needed services

Talk About Your Own Difficulties Managing Your Home. Your parent may be very aware that her lawn isn't mowed or that she is not taking the garbage down to the curb as often as she should—but she doesn't want to talk about it. So talk about your own lawn and your own pile of garbage. This will assure her that problems like this will not make you ship her off to the "old age home."

You might say: "Jeez, your lawn is looking a lot like mine. When I get home from work I'm just too tired to even think about getting out the lawn mower. It's a big job. As a matter of fact, I've been thinking about hiring a neighborhood kid to do it for me once a week. Have you ever thought of hiring someone?"

Talk About Other Elderly People Who Manage Their Own Homes.   It's reassuring for your parent to know that he isn't the only one who may need help if he wants to stay in his home. In casual conversation you can occasionally mention someone you know who has hired a homemaker or a home health aide. Talk about how pleased she is with the results. Build up the idea of in-home help as something lots of seniors are enjoying.

You might say: "Dad, did you know that Mr. Smith has someone come every day to help him do his household chores? Now that he has someone to help him do things like housecleaning, laundering, and shopping, his daughter says he doesn't worry anymore about having to sell his house and move into some kind of assisted living facility."

Talk About Gift Certificates for Needed Services.   Sometimes it is difficult for your parent to take the leap and ask for help. You can introduce the idea of assistance by giving her a service gift certificate. As a present, buy her gift certificates for a local food delivery service or the car wash or a housecleaning service. It's hard for her to turn down a gift, and if she actually uses it, she may find out that getting help is a good thing.

You might say: "I bought you this gift certificate for a shopping service. My friends use this, and they love it. This company will take your food order over the phone and deliver the food right to your door. Give it a try and let me know how you like it—I might try it myself."

Addressing Specific Issues
Talking about in-home care should be a give-and-take dialogue in which you and your parent both express your concerns and feelings. If he is in sound mental and physical health, you can't dictate what he must do and how he must live—but you can encourage him to think about all the different services that can make his life easier and safer.

After you get your parent used to the idea that asking for help is not such a bad thing, you can go into the details about the specific kinds of help available. You might talk about these topics:

- Home safety
- The different types of home care
- Finding the right service
- The cost of home care

Talk About Home Safety. The best way to keep your parent safe from accidents and injuries is to prevent them in the first place. It's a good idea to talk to your parent about safety hazards and ways to eliminate, correct, or avoid them.

You might say: "I just read that the most common injury in the home that causes older people to move into a nursing home is a broken hip. I know you don't want to have to leave this house, so it would be a good idea to make sure there are no safety hazards that could cause you to fall. Let's walk around the house together and see what we find."

You might say: "You know I worry about you when you're alone. I'd feel much better if I knew there were no safety hazards in the house. Would you mind if I just looked around a little bit for some problem areas that I recently read can make it more difficult for seniors to live safely on their own?"

When you give your parent's home a safety inspection, keep the following checklist handy. The Federal Trade Commission along with the American Association for Retired Persons (AARP) recommends that you look for these problem areas:

- Throughout the home
  Are handrails securely fastened on both sides of all stairways?
  Are all areas, including stairways, well lit? Are switches easy to operate?
  Do outside lights illuminate entrances and exits?
  Is a telephone accessible at all times? You may want to suggest a cordless telephone with charger.
  Are outside doors protected by security locks that can be easily operated?
  Are smoke detectors and carbon monoxide detectors strategically located?
  Are batteries replaced on a regular basis?
  Are floors and stairs kept free of cords and loose objects?
- Bathroom
  Is safety equipment properly installed? The basics are grab bars for the tub and shower and near the toilet.
  Do the tub and shower have no-slip surfaces?

Is the hot water heater set to prevent scalding?

Can you remove tripping hazards, such as cords and throw rugs?

Is there a night-light?

- Bedroom
  Is there a sturdy bedside table with a nontip lamp and space for eyeglasses?

  Does furniture placement allow a clear path between the bathroom and bedroom?

  Do rugs have nonslip backing?

  Is there a comfortable chair with arms for rest or comfort when dressing?

- Kitchen
  Can frequently used items be reached without using a chair or stool?

  Is a fire extinguisher within easy reach of the stove?

  Is there a work area where a person can sit while preparing food?

Simple improvements you identify using the checklist are inexpensive, and they barely affect the appearance of the home—yet they can make all the difference in an aging person's ability to continue living at home.

If your parent has any health problems, a home evaluation by an occupational therapist also can be helpful. This health professional can identify ways to improve home safety, arrange resources, and modify the environment to compensate for specific disabilities. For example, home improvements for someone with severe arthritis could include installing lever-action faucets in sinks and tubs, replacing doorknobs with lever handles, equipping the kitchen with an undercabinet jar opener and electric can opener and replacing knobs or small handles on cupboards and drawers with larger "C" handles.

Talk About the Different Types of Home Care.   You may think you know exactly what kind of help your parent needs to live safely and comfortably, but it's very important to ask him what he thinks. If he doesn't mind the dust all over the house, you will not convince him that he needs a housekeeper. If he resists your suggestions, you may need to remind yourself that no one has ever died of dirt and that perhaps preserving his privacy is more important to your parent than having an immaculate house. It's helpful to tell him what's available, how these services can help him, and how to get in touch with them, but after that it's your parent's call.

To begin, talk to your parent about her problem areas. Some older people need only a little help with shopping to be able to live at home; others need ongoing medical and personal care. Still others may need a mix of services, such as a housekeeping or chore service; cooking and meal preparation; transportation; and home health, rehabilitative therapy, or other medical care. You may find that your parent simply needs company and would benefit from social contacts she'll find at local senior centers.

You might say: "Staying in your own home is a good idea, but it's always nice to have some help with a big place like this. When I'm not around to help you, there are different types of services we can call on depending on what you need exactly. What services do you think would make your life easier?"

As you begin to take stock of the kinds of services your parent needs, help him choose the type of home care that would best give him this support. *Home- and community-based services* refers to the whole array of supportive services that help older persons live independently in their homes and communities. These services are provided by nonprofit organizations sponsored by religious or fraternal groups or other community organizations, and increasingly by commercial companies, many of which are doing a very good job. There are innumerable services for the elderly that vary in name and structure from state to state, but generally speaking they can all be categorized into four basic types:

- Homemaker services
- Home health services
- Adult day care services
- Community services

Homemaker Services.   The agencies that provide homemaker care for the elderly are also called home care agencies. They will help the elderly with what are called the instrumental activities of daily living: grocery shopping, transportation, household chores, snow removal, and leaf raking—the things that must be done to maintain independent living in a house or apartment. Homemaker agencies may or may not be licensed, depending on the state in which the agency operates.

Home Health Services.   Home health services (also called home health care or in-home care services) offer a variety of health services that are administered at the individual's home. They give assistance with activities of daily living such as bathing, eating, dressing, and toileting. And they provide health services that can include nursing care, administration of medications, and therapeutic care. Home health agencies may deliver intravenous medicine or nutritional supplements and may provide necessary medical equipment such as home oxygen equipment or wheelchairs. These agencies are strictly regulated by state and federal laws, and administer their services via physicians, social workers, nurses, and therapists. According to the National Association for Home Care, over twenty thousand home care agencies exist in the United States.

Adult Day Care Services. Adult day care services provide daily, structured programs in a community setting. Some of these offer daytime services that are strictly social, in a supervised environment. Others also offer health-related and rehabilitation services during daytime hours to the elderly who are physically or emotionally disabled and need a protective environment. These services are administered in nursing homes, assisted living residences, and other care facilities. Services can include physical, occupational, and speech therapy; meals, social activities (such as crafts, music, movies, community projects), transportation, companionship, and assistance with personal care needs such as bathing, eating, dressing, and grooming. Medically related services may be provided by health care professionals, including registered nurses and therapists; social workers and other staff attend to the general and social activities. The National Council on the Aging estimates that there are more than three thousand adult day care centers operating in the United States, about 90 percent of which are nonprofit or public.

These centers are very helpful to families who have an elderly parent who needs supervision and stimulation during the day. Adult day care allows the family members to continue working during daytime hours; it also gives families temporary relief from the responsibility of caring for older persons who are unable to care for themselves.

Community Services. There may be many services offered in your parent's community that can help her maintain her independence. These services may include the following:

- Senior centers. These facilities often offer classes, recreational opportunities, travel, volunteer opportunities, flu shots, and meals. They also provide social activities and companionship.

- Companion programs. Sometimes community groups sponsor programs in which volunteers visit isolated seniors in their homes to chat and check on their well-being. These are often called friendly visitor programs.

- Telephone reassurance. Some volunteer organizations and agencies for the elderly provide regular prescheduled calls to the homebound. This reduces social isolation and offers a routine safety check.

- Meal programs. Older people who are homebound may receive meal delivery through a Meals-on-Wheels program or private food service business. The meals are typically delivered at noontime Monday through Friday; some programs will also deliver on weekends. Some services will deliver a frozen meal that can be heated up for dinner.

- Gatekeeper programs. Some public utilities and the U.S. Postal Service offer gatekeeper programs in which service people who regularly visit the home are trained to notice anything unusual or any indication of need and to report it for investigation and action. If this service is active in your community, you might alert the program director to the fact that your parent is elderly and living alone.

- Energy assistance and weatherization. Home energy assistance and protective home repair assistance are available in most states to assist eligible families in paying their fuel bills or weatherizing their homes (insulation, caulking, storm windows, and so on).

- Emergency response systems. These are electronic devices

linking an individual to a fire department, hospital, or other health facility or social service agency. Simply pressing a button triggers a communicator attached to the telephone, which automatically dials the response center.

Talk About Finding the Right Service.   A good place to start your hunt for the right service would be to access the Eldercare Locator. (See the Resources section at the end of this chapter for the telephone number and Web address.) This is a nationwide, toll-free assistance directory sponsored by the Administration on Aging. It will give you the names of local organizations that offer health care and other services for older adults; it will also suggest services you may not even have thought of.

Talk About the Cost of Home Care.   Your parent will be concerned about the cost of these services that would allow him to stay in his own home. The price tag varies from community to community. In general you will find the following:

- Some long-term care insurance polices will cover in-home care.
- Medicaid will pay for some of the medically needy or those with low financial means.
- Medicare will pay for some very limited home care if the person has been discharged from a hospital and the care is prescribed by the physician.
- Some agencies charge on a sliding scale based on the person's ability to pay.
- Some agencies are private enterprises with set fees.

RESOURCES

American Association of Homes and Services for the Aging

This association represents not-for-profit organizations dedicated to providing high-quality health care, housing, and services to the nation's elderly. Its membership consists of over 5,000 not-for-profit nursing homes, continuing care retirement communities, and senior housing facilities, as well as assisted living and community services. AAHSA organizations serve more than one million older persons of all income levels, creeds, and races.

901 E Street NW
Washington, DC 20004
(202) 783-2242
www.aahsa.org

Eldercare Locator
(800) 677-1116 (weekdays 9 A.M. to 8 P.M. EST)
www.aoa.gov/elderpage/locator.html

This service offers a national toll-free number staffed by representatives who direct callers to the best source of information on services for the elderly in a local community.

National Association of Area Agencies on Aging (NAAAA)
927 Fifteenth NW, 6th floor
Washington, DC 20005
(202) 296-8130
www.n4a.org

The NAAAA provides information on locating community resources for older adults. They have published the *National Direc-*

tory for Eldercare Information and Referral. This directory provides the most complete listing available of local and state agencies on aging, as well as Native American aging programs. This popular item, distributed to over 2,000 aging service providers, associations, corporations, and Congress, is a leading resource for purchasers of products and services for the mature market. For further information, call (202) 296-8130.

National Association for Home Care
228 Seventh Street SE
Washington, DC 20003
(202) 547-7424
www.nahc.org

National Meals-on-Wheels Foundation
2675 Forty-Fourth Street SW, #305
Grand Rapids, MI 49509
(800) 999-6262

EXPERT HELP

This chapter was written with the expert help of Angela Heath, a master's-level gerontologist with the National Association of Area Agencies on Aging in Washington, D.C.

Alternative Living Arrangements

All research that's ever been done on this subject reveals what we already know: people want to stay in their own homes as long as possible. But the reality is that there are circumstances that will preclude this as a possibility.

Elinor Ginzler, AARP manager of long-term care and independent living, Washington, D.C.

Elisa is worried because her mother refuses to move from her home into a nursing home. "My mother is eighty-six years old and has been living alone since my father died ten years ago. She is a very proud and independent woman," says Elisa with tears welling in her eyes. "She doesn't want to move into any kind of senior citizen home or facility, but I really don't think she has any choice. Her last stroke left her partially paralyzed. She's in a wheelchair and needs twenty-four-hour care. I just don't know how to make her see that all her needs could be better taken care of if she would move to some kind of nursing home."

Kent, in contrast, is worried because his mother *wants* to move into a senior citizen home. "I can't believe she wants to sell her home and move into one of those assisted living communities," says Kent, shaking his head. "I know it's getting harder for her to manage on her own, but she could hire help. How can she just leave behind this beautiful house and all the memories that are here and live in a little apartment? I just don't get it. I told her she was making a big mistake that she'd regret, but she's doing it anyway."

Elisa and Kent are both worried about where their parents should live. After all, our parents' living arrangements can dictate how their health needs are met, the quality of life they enjoy, the social opportunities they have, and, in the very practical sense, how their money will be spent. These are major issues that are affecting the elderly and their families across the country.

A report issued by the National Institutes of Health says that about 35 percent of people reaching age sixty-five will have at least one nursing home admission during their lifetime. This is a large number of people that does not even include the millions of others who will move from their homes into their children's homes, into independent adult communities, or into some form of assisted living facility. Each one of these moves involves a difficult time of transition both for the parents and for their adult children. You have to be willing to talk about the possibility of such a move, the difficulties that are bound to exist, and the support you will offer.

This chapter discusses the reasons why you should have a conversation with your parent about where she would like to live if she should ever want to or have to move out of her home. It explores the best times to have this conversation and gives you the facts that will help you intelligently discuss the many options available for senior out-of-home living.

WHY TALK ABOUT ALTERNATIVE LIVING ARRANGEMENTS

John's mother had been living alone for twenty years in the home where John was raised. It never occurred to her or to John that she would live anywhere else. She liked the neighborhood and felt very comfortable among all her own things and the many memories that lived in that house. The neighbors loved her and looked in on her often. John had hired a lawn maintenance service, and the Meals-on-Wheels program brought her nutritious food almost every day. Why on earth would they talk about moving anywhere else?

John found out the hard way that this was a conversation he should have had with his mother just in case it ever became necessary to move. "Oh no," she'd certainly say to him, "I'm never leaving my home." But just the same, if John had encouraged her to talk about the possibility of moving, maybe it would have made the decision to put her in a nursing home an easier one. "When Mom was finally diagnosed with Alzheimer's disease," remembers John, "I didn't know what to do. Should I put her in a nursing home? Should I hire in-home help? Would she want to live in my house? Should she move to a nursing home near me or one near her friends at home? I tried to get her to make these decisions, but she just couldn't. She was too upset and confused to make these kinds of life-altering choices. I'm afraid I wasn't in much better shape, because I really had no idea where she wanted to live the last years of her life."

Change is difficult for everyone, especially for the elderly, who may feel they have already lost control over much of their lives. But, like all of us, if they are actively involved in the process of change, if they know in advance what the change will involve, if they are given the opportunity to make the decisions which guide that change, they can better adapt and make the change a positive one.

When you talk to your parent about future living arrangements, you give him two priceless gifts: the very precious opportunity to tell you his wishes before a crisis takes control out of his
hands, and the peace of mind that accompanies knowing that this
is a subject you can both talk about logically and with love.

WHEN TO TALK ABOUT ALTERNATIVE LIVING ARRANGEMENTS

Any day, any time is a good time to talk about alternative living
arrangements that your parents might consider in the future, but it's
a good idea to bring up the subject in these three situations at the
very least:

- Before a crisis
- Before it's a surprise
- Before a small problem gets worse

Before a Crisis

Guy's seventy-eight-year-old father broke his hip when he fell down
the front porch steps as he was walking out to pick up his newspaper. He was rushed to the hospital for surgery and was then transferred to the rehabilitation unit for one month of physical therapy.
Guy thought his dad was doing very well considering the severity of
the break, but then he got a call from a hospital representative who
informed him that his dad could not live by himself anymore and
was being discharged in forty-eight hours. "It had never occurred to
me," admits Guy, "that I would have to find my father someplace to
live. I couldn't think straight—I had no idea what he would like or
what he could afford."

Obviously Guy and his dad needed to talk, but there was no way around the fact that this was going to be a very hard transition. When you have to find alternative housing for your parent in the middle of a crisis, you have to deal with the stress over the lack of time, the stress of the physical problem, the stress of an elderly person who has just gone through a medical crisis, the stress of having to choose which personal items your parent would like to transfer to the new home and what to do with the rest of the things. Guy is lucky because his father is capable of making his wishes known, but in situations like those following a stroke, for example, the elderly person may not be able to communicate. The choice of an alternative living arrangement then falls on the family members, who may be unsure or in disagreement, or who may live too far away to invest the time needed for "shopping around," or who may be too upset by the medical crisis to make sound decisions. It is very difficult to know what's best if you haven't asked your parents in advance what they want.

Before It's a Surprise

Sixty-nine-year-old Rosemary and her seventy-four-year-old husband Jake were ready to move out of the family home they had lived in for fifty years. They just couldn't keep up with the maintenance and the bills, and they were feeling kind of lonely now that their lifelong neighbors had moved away or died. They were ready to make a change in their lives, so they called a real estate agent, put the house up for sale, and found an adult community they loved, down south in warmer weather. The move was well planned and thought out, but they omitted one small detail: they did not tell their three daughters about their plans until after the papers were signed and sealed. Rosemary and Jake announced their news as they sat around the holiday dinner table in the family dining room for

the last time with their three daughters and their families. The surprise caught the girls off guard; they all had the same reaction: "Oh,
no! How can you do this?" Rosemary and Jake had dropped lots of
hints that they were unhappy living in the big house, but nobody
had ever wanted to really talk about it. Now there were hard feelings
all around. "You could have at least told us what you were planning
before you signed the papers," cried one daughter. "You could have
at least asked us if we needed any help taking care of this house," shot
back her father. "Or how we felt being the old-timers in our own
neighborhood," sobbed the mother. This is a case where everyone
wanted everybody else to talk, but nobody made the first move.

Usually, before seniors pack up and move south, there are signs
of unrest. Don't be afraid to talk to your parents about their housing needs when you can see that they are starting to feel uncomfortable in their own home. They may have trouble with the bills;
they may feel "lost" in a big home; they may be lonely if they're isolated from social activities. When they hint around about these
kinds of problems, take the opportunity to talk to them about the
possibility of moving to another location. Let them know that you're
open to talking about the subject.

Before a Small Problem Gets Worse

The decision to move out of the family home usually evolves
over time as it becomes more and more difficult to manage alone.
A good time to talk about housing options is when you see signs of
problems that you know are only going to get worse. These signs
of difficulty are often noticeable during the holidays when you
return to your parent's home and see changes that worry you. You
may notice that the house itself is falling into disrepair. Or you may
notice a decline in the functioning level of your parent. Any of

these observations signal the need to talk about the future before you land in a crisis situation.

Look over this list of eight areas in which some elderly people need assistance; if your parent has problems in any of these areas, it may mean that she is having trouble living independently. Every no answer signals the possibility that your parent could benefit from a move to a more supervised environment:

- Mobility
  Can your parent move around easily?
  Can he effectively navigate with his cane, walker, or wheel-chair?
  Do you think he is mobile enough to keep up with the activities of daily living (eating, dressing, toileting, and the like)?
- Nutrition
  Can your parent prepare meals? Does she?
  Does she go shopping for food regularly, or has she made arrangements to have food delivered to her?
- Hygiene
  Does your parent take care of his personal needs, including bathing, shaving, and dressing?
  Does he give his time and attention to personal hygiene needs?
- Housekeeping
  Can your parent keep up with housekeeping chores, such as vacuuming, cleaning, laundry, changing linens?
  Is she willing to hire someone to come into the house to help out if she needs help?
- Toileting
  Is your parent able use the toilet without physical assistance on a regular basis?

Is he able and willing to manage his own incontinence,
colostomy, or catheter through proper use of supplies?
- Medications
Does your parent know when and how to take each medication?
Can she take her medications correctly without supervision?
- Mental status
Does your parent have the mental capacity to reason and to
plan and organize daily events?
Is she generally free of problems with anxiety, social with-
drawal, or depression?
Is her memory in pretty good shape?
Can she follow directions?
- Behavioral status
Is your parent able to cope with his feelings of depression,
anger, or fear?
Does he refrain from outbursts of anxiety or agitation?
Are you sure his actions pose no physical danger to himself or
others?

WHAT YOU SHOULD TALK ABOUT

What you will say to your parent about his future living arrangements of course depends on his health, finances, and personal situation. But as you think over the things you want to talk about, you
might keep the following suggestions in mind.

Breaking the Ice
The subject of alternative living arrangements is not an easy one to
bring up. It's usually not best to jump right into a conversation that
starts, "So Mom, if you have to move to a nursing home, which one

in this area do you particularly like?" Instead, you can broach the subject in a more casual and sensitive manner by following the guidelines in this section:

- Talk about other people
- Talk first about your own concerns
- Talk *with* your parent, not *at* him

Talk About Other People.   It's easy to start a conversation about alternative living arrangements by talking about somebody else. Use a third-party story that shows your parent why it is important to have this conversation before there's no time to talk about options.

You might say: "My neighbor just had a horrible experience with her dad. She had to find a place for him to live after he had a stroke, and she ran into all kinds of problems. It was very difficult on such short notice to find the right facility with the right medical care at the right price and at the same time find one that her dad would like. It really makes me stop and think. We should talk about this."

Talk First About Your Own Concerns.   Emphasize your concern rather than your parent's problems. Use "I" statements that focus first on your feelings before you tell your parent what you think she should do.

Instead of saying: "It's obvious that you're not able to take care of yourself or this house. I think you should move to a place where you don't have to do household work or worry about things like laundry and housework."
You might say: "I'm feeling worried because I can see that it's difficult for you to take care of yourself and the house. I'm wondering if this bothers you too."

You might say: "I worry about you living here alone. I've been wondering if you would like to move to a safer neighborhood that's closer to me and your grandchildren."

Talk with Your Parent, Not at Him.   Once you and your parent agree that it's time to look into alternative living arrangements, don't take over the search and try to dictate where your parent should live. Even if you're the one paying the bills, your parent needs to be actively involved in the decision-making process about where he will live.

Instead of saying: "I'll find a good place for you."
You might say: "Do you have any ideas about the type of place you'd like to live in?"

Instead of saying: "I've spent a lot of time researching adult community homes, and I've found one I know you're going to love."
You might say: "I've found ten adult community homes right in your area. Let's go visit them, and you can pick out the one that seems best for you."

Instead of saying: "Don't worry. I'll take care of everything."
You might say: "Together we'll find a place that you'll really like."

Addressing Specific Issues
There are many specific details involved in moving from home. The following are some of the most common topics of conversation; this section gives you a glimpse at how you can handle them:

- Difficulties at home
- A surprise move
- Household furnishings

- Moving your parent into your own home
- Types of alternative living facilities

Talk About Difficulties at Home.   When you notice that your parent is having some difficulty maintaining self or household, plan to talk about it. If you see signs of decline when visiting for the holidays, it's not always best to blurt out your concerns over the holiday meal, but you do want to make a mental note to say something before you leave.

You might say: "I really want to talk about something that I think is important. I'd like to get together with you some day next week."

You might say: "It's so difficult to keep up a home. How do you manage it all by yourself?"

You might say: "Have you ever thought about moving to a place where you don't have to work so hard to keep up the house and the housekeeping, like some kind of senior citizen facility?"

Talk About a Surprise Move.   If your parents should announce that they are going to move, find out what they want to do and ask open-ended questions to find out if they've thought this decision through.

Instead of saying: "Oh no! You can't sell your house and move to a senior citizen home!"
You might say: "This is a surprise. Tell me about your plans."

Without being judgmental, help them think about the details.

You might say: "It sounds like this is something you really want to do. What are the details? Will you have a kitchen where you can cook your own meals? What kind of social activities does this facility have? Is there any kind of medical care or supervision available if you should need it? Do you pay a rental fee every month, or is there a large up-front fee?"

If you disagree with their plans, say so, but don't slam shut the doors of communication.

You might say: "I don't understand your decision, and I'm not convinced it's the best thing for you. But if you're sure this is what you really want, I'd like to help you. Let me know if there's anything I can do."

Talk About Household Furnishings. Once the decision to move has been made, talk to your parents about what to do with all the furniture and items collected over a lifetime that will not fit in the new housing unit. Your parents should be directly involved in those decisions.

You might say: "I know you must feel a great sense of loss because you have to leave so much behind. Let me help you go through the things you've stored away. I'll bet there are a lot of good memories around here that would be fun to share. It'll also be best if you think about which items you'd like me to keep and which ones you'd like to give away or discard. I don't want you to do this alone, and I don't feel comfortable making those decisions, so let's do it together."

Talk About Moving Your Parent into Your Own Home. Your own home is one of the alternative housing options you might consider when you realize your parent can no longer live on his own. Before you offer this option, however, it is always best to talk it over with everyone who lives in your house. A family crisis may be in the making if, for example, an adult daughter assumes that her husband and children will have no problem with her mom moving in with them. In order for this decision to work, it has to be a family decision. Everyone may not cheer loudly about the idea, but they need to have an opportunity to discuss it and examine what needs to be done to make this arrangement work or to talk about the reasons why it cannot work.

Talk together about the facts: Do you have the room to comfortably accommodate the privacy needs of your parent? How does everyone feel about sharing the household? What kind of relationship do you have with your parent—is it one in which both of you can peacefully coexist under the same roof? How much care does your parent need? Can she live independently? How much assistance does she need? Is it assistance that you can realistically provide? What will happen if she needs more care? The answers to these questions will help you separate what you wish you could do from what you realistically can do.

If all family members feel that bringing an elderly parent into the home is a good idea, then you should offer the option to your parent. But don't expect an immediate outpouring of thanks and gratitude. Although moving into your home is an option that may be emotionally easier on your parent than moving into a senior facility, it still involves loss—loss of total independence, loss of personal space, loss of personal items like furniture and wall hangings. This is a gracious offer on your part, but it's still an option that your parent may need time to think about. So don't take it as an insult if your parent doesn't jump at the idea.

You might say: "Dad, Mary and I are worried about you living alone. We've talked it over, and we agree that we would love to have you move into our home. But it's something that I know would be a major life change for you, so I just wanted to plant the seed, let you know you're welcome, and ask you to think it over."

Assure your parent that you realize a move like this can be stressful for everyone, but once you're sure this is what you want to do, emphasize the positive.

You might say: "Dad, you have so much to offer our family. You can help me watch after the kids, and you can share your love of art and music with all of us. I'm really looking forward to moving your favorite things into the spare bedroom."

Your parent may have lots of questions that he is afraid to ask. It's better to have all concerns addressed before the move, so encourage your parent to talk about any reservations, concerns, or practical issues.

You might say: "I know this is a hard decision to make, and you probably have a lot of questions about where and how you would live. So let's talk about that."

If you've decided that care in your home is appropriate, you'll probably need to make some changes around the house. Changes can be as complex as adding another bathroom or converting a first-floor den into a bedroom, or as simple as attaching a safety rail to the shower stall or installing an amplified receiver on the telephone. Here are a few examples to get you started thinking:

- Install a help alert system.
- Remove clutter, sharp objects, and throw rugs.
- Install nonskid strips in showers and bathtubs.
- Place a flashlight by the bed.
- Install night-lights in halls and bathrooms.
- Install railings next to all stairways and steps.

- Set the hot water heater to a lower temperature.
- Take a certified CPR course.

In addition, you'll want to make your loved one feel welcome in your home by displaying his favorite possessions—particularly mementos and photographs—in plain sight.

If you talk about these details, caring for an aging loved one in your own home may be not only the most practical choice in your situation but also the most rewarding.

Talk About Types of Alternative Living Facilities. If it is not feasible to have your parent move into your home, there are several types of alternative living facilities that are appropriate for seniors at different stages of independence and dependence. They offer a range of services and support. To help your parent choose the type of facility that best fits her needs, talk about the services and amenities she would like; you may find the following questions useful:

Do you want a facility that has a flexible schedule or one that is more structured?

Are there certain pieces of furniture and personal belongings you would like to be able to bring with you?

Do you want to stay geographically near family and friends?

Do you want a facility that offers recreational activities, social programs, and group outings?

Would you like to be in a high-security facility?

Would you prefer a facility that provides transportation to doctors, shopping, and other places?

Do you want a facility that serves meals, or would you rather be able to cook your own meals?

Do you want a facility that can help you with basic activities of daily living like bathing, dressing, eating, and toileting?

When you have an idea of the type of lifestyle your parent is looking for, you can begin to talk about the different kinds of senior living arrangements. These are the most common types:

- Independent living facilities
- Assisted living communities
- Nursing homes
- Continuing care retirement communities

The descriptions that follow will help you talk to your parent about her options.

Independent Living Facilities.   Independent living arrangements include senior apartments and congregate senior housing. In both of these living arrangements, the senior citizen leads an independent lifestyle that requires minimal or no extra help. These apartments are most appropriate for seniors who are able to walk without assistance and prefer living in an environment where there are other seniors.

- Senior apartments. These rental units are part of a building development restricted for lease to seniors only. Many senior citizens enjoy living in an environment free of children and young adults. They like living where they are near others of the same generation and can more easily make friends. These housing complexes do not include services like meals, transportation, or social activities.

- Congregate senior housing. Also called a retirement home or community, this is a multiunit senior housing development that is paid for on a monthly basis. The fee usually includes supportive services, such as meals, housekeeping, social activities, and transportation. Other typical services include laundry and linen service, dining room, emergency call system, controlled access, and social services.

Assisted Living Communities. Assisted living communities are group residential facilities that provide for daily meals, personal and other supportive services, health care, and twenty-four-hour supervision. Also called personal care, residential care, or domiciliary care facilities, this type of living arrangement strives to give seniors as much privacy and autonomy as possible. Such a facility is most appropriate for senior citizens who need some assistance with activities of daily living, such as dressing, eating, or bathing, but who don't need the level of medical care provided in nursing homes. The sizes and types of assisted living communities vary widely; services provided range from meals and housekeeping to medication assistance, incontinence care, and limited nursing service. According to the American Association of Homes and Services for the Aging, the assisted living industry is the fastest-growing segment of the senior housing industry; more than one million seniors live in this type of residence.

Assisted living care is generally paid for through private funds, Supplemental Security Income (SSI), or long-term care insurance policies. Medicare does not pay for assisted living. Medicaid coverage varies from state to state, but rarely covers assisted living costs.

Nursing Homes. A nursing home is a facility that provides twenty-four-hour nursing care for seniors with long-term care needs. Regular medical supervision and rehabilitation therapy are typically available; additional services such as subacute care, intravenous therapy, physical therapy, and respiratory therapy may also be available. The better homes offer a full array of nursing and personal assistance, dietary, therapeutic, social, and recreational services. Meals, laundry, housekeeping, and medical services should also be provided. Some nursing homes have dedicated sections for residents with Alzheimer's disease; other nursing home facilities have been built specifically for this purpose. In any case, if your parent has Alzheimer's, the nursing home should be equipped and staffed specifically to deal with this disease.

Nursing homes are also called skilled nursing facilities, convalescent homes, nursing facilities, and long-term care facilities. Nursing homes are licensed by each state according to federal guidelines. The cost of nursing home residence is generally paid through private funds, Medicaid, Medicare (short-term only), or long-term care insurance.

Continuing Care Retirement Communities (CCRCs).   These facilities offer a complete range of housing and health care accommodations, from independent living to twenty-four-hour skilled nursing care. Residents enter as healthy, independent seniors and move from one level of care to another as their needs change. CCRCs are for older adults who want the security of knowing that as they age, most of their long-term health care needs will be met within the retirement community without the need to relocate. Many CCRCs require a large deposit prior to admission and charge monthly fees thereafter. These costs are paid from the person's private funds.

Licensing requirements for senior citizen housing vary from state to state. You should check with your State Agency on Aging to find out what standards apply to each type of housing and how you can be sure that the facilities you are interested in have the necessary licenses and certifications.

If you could not live in your own home during the last years of your life, where would you like to live? Obviously, this is a big decision that you would not want made quickly, carelessly, or without your input. Your parents surely feel the same way. If they are at all open to discussing this topic, you can give them the information and support to help make a difficult decision just a little easier.

RESOURCES

American Association of Retired Persons (AARP)
601 E Street NW
Washington, DC 20049
(800) 424-3410
www.aarp.org

AARP offers assistance to the general public in finding alternative care. The organization's publications and Web materials will help you make informed and educated choices.

The American Association of Homes and Services for the Aging (AAHSA) offers the *Consumer's Directory of Continuing Care Retirement Communities*, with listings of close to five hundred facilities nationally. This directory will help you choose the CCRC that's right for your parent. For more information about purchasing this directory, visit the AAHSA website at www.aahsa.org, or contact AAHSA Publications at (800) 508-9442.

Senior Sites
www.seniorsites.com

Senior Sites is the most comprehensive Web source of information about nonprofit housing and services for seniors. With over five thousand listed communities, Senior Sites is a valuable resource for seniors and their families interested in exploring the nonprofit housing option. In addition, Senior Sites includes information to guide you in selecting a nonprofit housing facility, links to websites with senior housing resources, and a directory of national and state senior housing associations.

Eldercare Locator
(800) 677-1116 (weekdays 9 A.M. to 8 P.M. EST)
www.aoa.gov/elderpage/locator.html

This service offers a national toll-free number staffed by representatives who direct callers to the best source of information on services for the elderly in a local community.

EXPERT HELP

This chapter was written with the expert help of Elinor Ginzler, AARP manager of long-term care and independent living in Washington, D.C. In this position, Ginzler maintains a strong leadership role in planning for the association's information and education activities on the issues of long-term care and independent living. She oversees the work of AARP on designing and implementing initiatives to provide members with information products and services to maximize their options as their needs and circumstances change. Staff under her direction maintain expertise in such areas as assisted living, nursing home quality, assistive devices, universal design and home modifications, transportation, and home- and community-based services.

Part Four

Financial Issues

Daily Money Management

Adult children have a responsibility to be aware of issues that might be affecting their parents' finances.
Robert O. Weagley, Ph.D., associate professor
of consumer and family economics at the
University of Missouri-Columbia

When Trisha was young, her parents felt it was important to teach her how to handle her money carefully. "I remember the day I counted up the profits from my lemonade stand," she says, "and my mom took me to the bank to open my first savings account. I was so proud to have my own passbook and to be in charge of my own money."

Later, when Trisha graduated from lemonade stands to baby-sitting, she was allowed to keep one-half of her earnings, but her parents made sure that the other half went right into the bank. Her parents also taught the lessons of money management by example. They waited for big-ticket items to go on sale; they shopped at discount stores; and they rarely splurged on "unnecessary luxuries."

Because her parents had always been so very careful with money, Trisha was shocked when her mother announced that she was taking out an equity loan against the value of her house to throw an extravagant party for her friend's seventieth birthday. "This was so unlike my mother. I felt she was making a major mistake, but I wasn't sure if it was any of my business to tell her what to do with her money."

This is a hard question to answer: Is it your business how your parents spend their money? If your parents are financially secure and have a trusted financial adviser, they probably don't need your advice. But as they get older and you see subtle signs that they are beginning to lose their mental sharpness, or if they are at all financially shaky to begin with, or if they suddenly and radically change their spending habits—the experts say that yes, it absolutely is your business. The family, they feel, has to be like a team. Everyone should look after each other's best interests, and as parents age, adult children have to step up to take on more responsibility to make sure these family members are financially safe and protected. This is not advocating overt meddling, but it does require an ongoing awareness of what's going on in situations that might be affecting the parents' finances.

This chapter helps you decide when you should talk to your parents about the way they manage their money. It explains why they sometimes need financial guidance and details symptoms of financial problems that indicate it is time to talk. It gives you the words you need to break the ice and to address some specific money issues, and helps you decide what to do and say if you find that your parents are unable to handle their own money.

WHY TALK ABOUT MONEY MANAGEMENT

As adult children, we should talk to our elderly parents about their methods of money management because managing money after retirement can be difficult, and mistakes can be life altering. In particular, this section shows you why it's important to ensure that

- There's enough money to live on
- The money is well managed
- Spending priorities are straight
- There are no health issues affecting sound money management
- Your parents are not being taken advantage of by exploitative or even criminal third parties

To Ensure That There's Enough Money to Live On
Retired older people who are living on a fixed income are faced with daily decisions about how to spend their money, pay their bills, and still enjoy a reasonable standard of living. In order to make sure that your parents have enough income to meet their needs, you should know where they get their money and if it is enough to support them. Those who are retired generally rely on such sources as Social Security payments, pensions from former employment situations, personal saving accounts, investments in stocks and bonds, veteran's benefits, or welfare payments. Where do your parents get their money? If they are relying on pensions, has the payment been adjusted to match inflation? If your father dies, do his pension payments transfer to your mother?

These are important questions to answer. It is not uncommon for elderly people who have worked hard all their lives to end up in silent poverty in their old age. The *U.S. Census Bureau Poverty*

Report 1998 (the last year for which these figures are available) tells us that the poverty rate among older people increases substantially with age. Among the population ages forty-five to fifty-four, 6.9 percent live in poverty. That number jumps to 10.5 percent after the age of sixty-five. These numbers tell us that we shouldn't assume our parents can afford to live comfortably. It's our responsibility to talk to them and find out.

To Ensure That the Money Is Well Managed

Times have changed in the financial market, but your parents may not be aware of all the options available to them nor comfortable exploring them. That's why you should have conversations that will help your parents understand various methods of money management. You should know if your parents have their money in high- or low-interest-bearing accounts. (It would not be unusual for them to have most of their money divided between a low-interest bank account and a large envelope under their mattress.) You should find out if they are collecting the benefits they are entitled to (from their pension or from the government, for example). You can talk to them about making secure investments that can make their money grow without endangering their financial future. (The elderly who suffered through the Depression are still often very leery of investing in the stock market.) Making sure your parents' money is well managed is insurance against a reduced standard of living in old age. We all need occasional financial guidance; who will give it to the elderly? Family members should be first in line.

To Ensure That Spending Priorities Are Straight

Top-of-the-list spending priorities are the same at any age. First, there must be enough money to buy food, shelter, clothing, and health care; then all of life's other expenditures follow. This reality helped Trisha decide to talk to her mother about the expensive party she was planning for her friend's birthday. Trisha knew that monthly loan payments would make money extremely tight, so she decided that it was her responsibility to advise her mother against this expense. It's not uncommon for the elderly to sacrifice their own needs to give to their friends, family, children, and grandchildren. It's also not unheard of to find elderly people "throwing their money away" on things they don't need at all (such as six cases of lightbulbs from a local fundraiser) and finding their food budget too quickly depleted. We need to talk to our parents if there's a chance that their spending habits may not leave them enough money for themselves.

To Ensure That There Are No Health Issues
Affecting Sound Money Management

Sometimes financial problems are the result of health problems. You'll want to talk to your parents about their monetary troubles if you suspect that their health insurance coverage is not adequate, thus causing their doctor and prescription bills to take too large a chunk out of their resources. You might also find that your parents will have additional money problems if they suffer from such health problems as substance abuse, dementia, or depression. The cost of treatment for these problems can disrupt any budget, and in addition, when financial judgment is weakened by these problems, the results can be disastrous.

Harold's experience is an unfortunately typical example of what can happen to a person's financial state when his mental faculties are compromised. Harold's adult children knew he was having a hard time adjusting to his retirement and was very unhappy, and they noticed that he was spending more and more of his time in the local bar. But they figured he just needed time to adjust to his new life. After awhile they began to worry about his physical health

because he wasn't eating and seemed quite depressed. What they
didn't even consider was what his new habits and routine might be
doing to his financial health. It turned out that when drunk, Harold
spent hundreds of dollars daily buying rounds of drinks for his new
friends. He lost several thousand dollars on the many betting pools
he entered, and he loaned $50,000 to a bar "friend" who was down
and out. His retirement fund was soon depleted, and his so-called
friends drifted away when the free drinks stopped. The fellow who
took the loan disappeared, and Harold was left alone and broke. His
children never saw it coming.

In addition to the dialogue suggestions you'll find in the chapters addressing specific problems such as alcoholism, dementia, and
depression, you should also talk about these situations that give you
reason to talk about the effect of these problems on your parents'
financial resources.

**To Ensure That Your Parents Are Not Being Taken
Advantage of by Exploitative or Even Criminal Third Parties**
Talking regularly with your parents about their methods of money
management makes it more difficult for unscrupulous people to con
them out of their money. Without the help of their families, senior
citizens become easy prey for scam artists because they tend to be
more trusting than younger people and often cave in to scam artists
who use high-pressure sales tactics.

Common scams involve home repair contractors and callers
seeking donations to fake charities. "Boiler-room" operations run by
fraudulent investment brokers also pounce on the fears of the
elderly. If a family member is not keeping an eye on an elderly person's finances, smooth-talking brokers can easily convince an eighty-
year-old person to put all her money in deals promising fast, high
returns on investments in penny stocks, bonds, art, coins, diamonds,

and such that put her finances at risk but give the broker a nice commission on the sale. See the chapter "Consumer Fraud" for more details on how to talk to your parents about this particular problem.

WHEN TO TALK ABOUT DAILY MONEY MANAGEMENT

Discussions about money management, investing, and spending require no special invitation or crisis. They can be a routine part of many daily conversations with your parents. However, when you do see symptoms of possible money problems, you should not waste time getting to the point. We discuss the following symptoms in this section:

- Lifestyle changes
- Possible misuse of retirement funds
- Trouble with bill payments
- Inadequate self-care
- New significant other is suddenly on the scene
- Inexplicable expenditures or grandiose schemes

When Your Parents Make Lifestyle Changes

Marian was shocked when her parents told her that they would not be renting the beach house at the shore this year. For the last thirty-five years, they had spent the first two weeks of July vacationing by the ocean—what could make them change their minds now? Thinking maybe they couldn't afford it anymore and were too proud to say so, Marian didn't push them for a reason. She tried to support their decision by agreeing that the area had become too crowded and that the weather hadn't been that great last year anyway. Unfortunately, however, by trying to let her parents save face, Marian was ignoring a major symptom of money problems that she should talk about with her parents.

Money management habits often dictate one's lifestyle. You know from long experience whether your parents love to spend money to socialize, vacation, and redecorate or whether, in contrast, they are stubbornly frugal and find ways to "get by" even when they could easily buy themselves a more comfortable existence. If you notice a sudden change in your parents' lifestyle that involves the way they spend money—becoming more miserly or more extravagant in their spending habits—this is a signal that something has happened, and you need to talk about it. You might find out that your dad has canceled his magazine and newspaper subscriptions. You might see that your mother no longer goes out for lunch with her friends. You might be surprised to find out that your parents have joined a tropical fruit club and are paying for crates of oranges and grapefruits they could never eat in a lifetime. Any sudden change in routine or habit may be a sign of financial difficulties or mismanagement.

In Marian's case, hearing that her parents had canceled their vacation plans was a good opportunity, first, for her and her siblings to thank their parents for all those years of free vacations by chipping in to pay the rent on the next trip. It also gave them a reason to open a dialogue about the difficult challenge of sound money management after retirement.

When There Is Possible Misuse of Retirement Funds

Frank's dad was more excited than he had been in years. Now that he was finally retired, he was going to do something exciting. Like a teenager with visions of his first car, Frank's dad explained that he was going to take one-third of his pension fund and buy a mobile home to enjoy his dream of making a cross-country tour. Frank knew this expenditure was a mistake but didn't want to dampen his father's enthusiasm. What could he say?

Upon retirement your parents may have many decisions to make about how to invest and use their money. This is a good time to talk about asset and money management. You might begin with casual conversations about other people who have retired and how they have managed their money (both the good and the bad) and then eventually guide the conversation specifically to your parents' plans. By discussing opportunities and options, you can help your parents explore what they will need money for throughout their years of retirement, where that money will come from, how much they want to spend, and how much they can invest. Careful planning can avoid their having a lower standard of living later when the retirement funds become depleted. A $100,000 retirement fund may seem like a lot to an older person, but in today's financial climate, that won't feed and shelter a person for very long. After retirement, many seniors will live for another twenty years or more!

In Frank's case, after listening to his dad's plans with shared enthusiasm and congratulating him on his plans to enjoy himself after putting in so many years of hard work, Frank encouraged his father to investigate all possible options for financing the trip. He suggested that it would be more financially sound to rent the vehicle and invest the remainder. Frank's dad admitted that in his excitement he hadn't thought of that possibility and would look into it. If you see your parents making a mistake with their retirement funds, don't just cross your fingers and hope for the best. Sometimes our parents are grateful to have someone who will listen to their plans for retirement and help them organize the financial details. If they're not looking for advice, at least you'll know you tried.

When Your Parents Have Trouble with Bill Payments

Cathy dropped by unexpectedly one Saturday morning to have a cup of tea with her mom. While the water was heating, she took a nostalgic look around her mother's living room where Cathy had grown up. The same old couch sat tiredly against the wall, the same lamp with its faded cover gave off its dim light in the corner, and the same little desk where her mother kept her correspondence stood near the door. Cathy's memories of years gone by were abruptly interrupted when she spied the stack of unopened letters on the desk. Looking closer, Cathy saw they were several months' worth of unpaid bills. She quickly turned away from the desk knowing her mother would be embarrassed, maybe even angry, if she saw Cathy looking through the letters. At the same time, Cathy felt she had to say something—but what?

Yes, adult children should talk to their parents when they know the bills are piling up. This is a symptom of a problem that may be financial or may even involve cognitive health. (And some seniors simply forget to pay their bills!) Whatever the reason, when bills go unpaid the consequences can be severe, so you certainly have the right to step in to help.

You might see stacks of bills piling up, or you might pick up from your parents' conversations that they are having trouble paying bills; you can also assume that they might be having problems if something has happened to cause an increase in their monthly bills—something like a hospital stay or a home renovation project. Those bills can be very confusing and can quickly become overwhelming. Double billing, overcharging, and misdirected bills happen to all of us, but these problems are especially confusing for the elderly.

Talk to your parents about the difficulty of keeping track of bill payments and offer to help them. Encourage them to let you review their checkbook, bank statements, and canceled checks. You'll know that you need to talk further about their financial state if you see any of the following:

- Inappropriate payments, such as payments for medical bills that have already been paid
- Numerous payments to credit card companies, home shopping networks, sweepstakes, or other contests
- Unusually large donations to charitable or fraternal organizations
- Failure to list or otherwise track deposits and checks
- Numerous transfers from savings to checking accounts
- Consistent or unusual payments to a person unknown to you

Cathy didn't say anything to her mother about the unopened bills in the hope of protecting her pride and independence. She soon learned that this decision was the wrong one when she had to run over to her mother's house about one month later because she was not able to get through on the telephone. She found her mother sitting on that old couch crying because the phone had been shut off, the public utility company was threatening to shut off her electricity, and the credit card company had handed her account over to a collection agency. Now in this crisis situation, Cathy sat down to talk to her mother about her financial situation.

When Your Parents Show Signs of Inadequate Self-Care
Greg was worried about his mother's vision. At the restaurant a week earlier, she had asked him to order for her—a request at odds with her independent personality. And now she wanted him to come over and read a letter she had received from her bank. She said she wasn't sure what the letter wanted her to do, but Greg suspected that she was having trouble reading it. Why, he wondered,

would someone who was generally very good about taking care of her health not go to the eye doctor if she needed new glasses?

The reason for Greg's mother's reluctance to see an eye doctor may be financial. As we all know, good personal care costs money. That's why if you see that your parents are neglecting some area of self-care, consider that it might be a symptom of financial problems. Adequate clothing—a warm coat, sturdy shoes, quality undergarments—can get expensive. Nutritional food too can put a crimp in a senior's budget. (Unfortunately, the stories about elderly people eating cat food are not exaggerations.) And of course, health care is extremely expensive when not covered by some form of insurance. As elderly people try to manage on a fixed income, their ability to afford the necessities of life can diminish. If you're alert to things like the quality of your parents' food, clothing, and health care, you'll notice when it seems they may be having a financial problem.

When Greg saw that his mother definitely was having trouble reading fine print in dim light, he didn't beat around the bush. He asked her directly why she didn't make an appointment with an eye doctor. After Greg rejected her excuses that she didn't have the time and didn't really have a problem anyway, she finally admitted that although her health insurance policy would pay for the eye exam, it did not cover new lenses or frames. She was worried that if she had to pay more than $50 for them she would not have enough money to pay her other monthly bills. If Greg had never asked, he never would have known that she needed his help for something so very important.

When a New Significant Other Is Suddenly on the Scene
"You what?!" Dede yelled over the phone line. She couldn't believe what her mother just told her. How could she run off and elope with this Stan whom she hardly even knew? Dede cautiously gave her

mother her best wishes, hung up the phone, and sat down and cried. Dede's mother was a wealthy woman, and Dede had often worried that some unscrupulous man might try to scam her out of her money—now it was very possible that the worst had happened. Maybe Stan was an honest man who really loved her mother, Dede thought, but then why the rush? At that moment Dede was kicking herself for not having had a good talk with her mother about how to protect her money.

There is good reason to talk to your parent about his finances when a new significant other suddenly arrives on the scene. Of course there's no reason to interfere in your parent's love life, but you certainly should inject the voice of sound judgment when you see a parent being swept off his feet by someone unknown to the family. The best time to talk about protecting family money and assets is before a romance begins, but if you haven't talked yet and you see love lights in your parent's eyes, it's important to have a good conversation about planning for future financial security.

When There Are Inexplicable Expenditures or Grandiose Schemes

Vicki's dad was a new man. He seemed to be finally getting over the death of his wife and was ready to get on with his life. In fact, he was making big plans to build a new home right on his favorite golf course down in the Bahamas. "It is time," he told his daughter, "to enjoy my life." To Vicki's way of thinking, enjoying life was one thing but blowing the bankroll and piling up debts at his age were something else all together. Vicki didn't want to pop her dad's bubble, but she wondered if he had gone over the edge and needed her to pull him back to the steady ground of reality.

What your parents do with their retirement money is their business, but if you see them overspending on grandiose schemes that will hurt their financial security, that's certainly an indicator that they may need a helping hand. This is a signal to you that you should broach the subject of future financial health and offer to help them set up a plan that would keep them financially secure in the years to come. Don't be afraid to step in with a few words of advice.

If Vicki had listened to her inner voice that told her she should say something to her father about his wild expenditures, he probably wouldn't be living in her basement right now, up to his eyeballs in debt with no resort home to show for it.

WHAT YOU SHOULD TALK ABOUT

In your conversations with your parents about their daily money management, you should try to be supportive and noncritical. It is their money, after all, and in most circumstances you can't dictate what they should or should not buy. But you can offer them bits of helpful information that will get them thinking about the subject on their own.

Breaking the Ice

You can get your parents to talk about their money more easily by talking first about your own. When you open up about the kind of day-to-day financial decisions you're making, you open a door to a discussion that can give you lots of information you can use to help your parents. Let's say you just got your car insurance statement in the mail. You might casually mention this to your dad, saying, "I'm thinking about raising the deductible on my car insurance policy to lower the premium. By the way, what kind of deductible are you carrying on your car?" You might find that your parent is still carrying a

$100 deductible (thinking this is all he wants to pay out-of-pocket in the event of an accident) without realizing that it's costing him about $250 extra a year for this possible "savings." Use your own experiences with creditors, investments, savings, and so on to lead into questions about your parents' financial position.

You might also use the financial circumstances of family and friends to open the door to a discussion about money. You might talk about your friend who is very worried about his parents because they are living on a fixed income yet spend most weekends in the casino. You might ask about the financial well-being of Aunt Tilly, who is retired on a teacher's pension. Then you can slide in a personal question, such as "I sometimes wonder how you and Mom are doing now that you're retired. Do you feel you have enough money to live comfortably?" Casual conversations are much better icebreakers than are direct confrontations.

Addressing Specific Issues

Money affects almost every aspect of our lives: what we eat, where we live, how we dress, how we socialize, and so on. In any aspect of daily living, you may see signs that your parents are having financial difficulties. The following dialogue suggestions will give you an idea of how you can approach a range of subjects without embarrassing or criticizing your parents' judgment. Specific things you might talk about include

- Your parents' standard of living
- Overspending
- Charge cards

Talk About Your Parents' Standard of Living. Are your parents spending enough money to maintain a reasonable standard of living?

By nature, some people become miserly as they get older and have to live on a fixed income. They fear running out of money; they fear becoming dependent on others; they fear diminishing their children's inheritance. If you keep your eyes open when you visit, your parents' day-to-day activities will reveal financial worries like these, giving you opportunities to bring them up in conversation.

You might say: "Dad, it must be tough to budget money now that you're retired. Do you find it difficult to do all the things you want to do or the things you're used to doing?"

You might say: "Mom, this refrigerator is really empty. How about you and I do some food shopping right now?"
If she resists, keep insisting and add: "Come on, I'll treat you to some of the food I know you've always loved."

If she then goes along, you'll have an inkling that her initial resistance was due to financial worries. While you're shopping, you might strike up a conversation about the high cost of food and how difficult it must be to keep a stock of fresh food on a fixed budget. This opens the door to a discussion of finances that is general and nonconfrontational.

You might say: "Dad, that coat has always looked good on you, but it's looking a little worn. I saw one that's a lot like it when I was shopping the other day. How about you and I go take a look at it? It's important to me that you look good and feel warm this winter."

You might say: "Mom, you've worked hard all your life, and now is the time to enjoy yourself a little. I want you to go out and buy yourself some new clothes. In fact, I'll go with you and treat you to lunch. How's next Saturday?"

Talk About Overspending. Overspending is a tough issue to talk about. If you see your parents "throwing their money away" and you step in and question what they're doing, it can look as though you're worried about losing the full value of your inheritance. This is especially difficult if you've never talked to them about money before or if you have been basically uninvolved in their lives up to this point. This difficulty gives you one more reason why it's so important to make money matters a common topic of discussion through the years so that in the event that your parents later dramatically change their spending habits it won't seem like such an intrusion if you question what they're doing.

You might say: "I saw this great leather coat I'd like to buy, but it's just so expensive it would throw my whole monthly budget off. How do you do it? How can you afford that new car and still keep yourself financially secure?"

This kind of questioning asks for advice while encouraging your parents to think about budgets and spending habits.

You might say: "I read this article about the number of senior citizens living in poverty. It must be so hard to work all your life and then not have enough money to live comfortably after you retire. Do you find it hard to budget your money?"

You're not asking your parents to account for their spending habits; you're just asking a general question that may get them thinking about how they spend their money.

You might say: "Mom, you might say it's none of my business, but I have to say something about the way you always pick up the whole bill every time you go out to lunch or dinner with your friends. I don't think your friends expect you to always pay, and I don't think you can afford to keep doing it. Why do you do that?"

Talk About Charge Cards. Debt is generally resolved when you borrow in the low-income years and pay it back in the high-income years. That's why credit is an issue that can get out of hand with seniors who no longer have potential income growth after retirement. If your parents' method of "budgeting" is to charge everything, you should step in and try to guide them into a more cash-centered spending pattern.

You might say: "I heard a financial adviser talking on the radio the other day, and he said that credit card debt for the elderly should be zero because after retirement there are no more high-income years yet to come, and the interest on credit is so very expensive. He felt that the card could be used all month long for its convenience but that it should be paid off completely at the end of each month. Would you find it tough to pay off what you charge each month?"

You might say: "I sometimes worry that I put too much on my charge card. The interest rate is so high, and it just kills my budget. Do you worry about your credit card debts?"

You might say: "Instead of charging that pair of shoes and paying such high interest rates, why don't you pay cash this time? It'll save you money in the long run."

You might say: "Pop, I'm worried about the way you seem to charge up a storm on your credit card every time you drink too much. You buy everybody in the room a round of drinks and then go charge some big-ticket item that you don't really need—like that big-screen TV you bought last week. If you keep drinking and charging, you're going to go broke. How about getting back on the wagon and into

AA again? I think it's really important to get this under control to save yourself from financial disaster."

TALKING ABOUT TAKING CHARGE

Jane watched with great concern and sadness as her dad made more and more financial mistakes. He often forgot to pay bills, or he paid them twice. He would make a cash withdrawal from the bank and have no idea where the money was by the time he got home. He would bring a week's worth of groceries to the checkout and find he had only a $5 bill in his pocket. He would grumble to her about the incompetence of the bankers and cashiers and even friends who tried to cheat him out of his money. He seemed to have no idea that he was the one with a problem. Then she got a call from a neighbor who had helped him get things straight when he paid for a newspaper with a $100 bill at the corner store, thinking it was a $1 bill. Jane knew she had to do something, but wasn't sure what. It's hard to tell parents that you don't think they are capable of keeping track of their own money.

If you find that your elderly parent is unable to manage her money, you should step in with one of two options:

1. Hiring a professional money manager
2. Taking over the responsibility for financial obligations and benefits yourself

Hiring a Professional Money Manager

The new field of daily money management for senior citizens provides services on a fee-for-service basis, usually $25 to $100 an hour. (To find a money manager, you can contact the American Association of Daily Money Managers listed in the Resources at the end of this chapter.) The services these money managers perform include the following:

- Organizing and keeping track of financial and medical records
- Establishing a budget
- Helping with check writing and checkbook balancing
- Serving as a representative payee or fiduciary with authority to administer the benefits of people who can't manage their own financial affairs

You might say: "Dad, I was thinking about how difficult it must be for you to constantly keep track of all your finances. There's so much to do and remember. That's why I've set up an appointment for us to talk to a financial adviser. They now have these wonderful services to help senior citizens that I thought would be interesting to learn more about."

Make sure your parents know that you are not trying to grab hold of their money or assets.

You might say: "No one is going to tell you how you can or cannot spend your money; this arrangement simply makes it easier for you to keep track of expenses, bills, and the like."

Taking Over the Responsibility for Financial Obligations and Benefits Yourself

If you decide to step in yourself and take over your parent's finances, you will need to contact a lawyer to obtain power of attorney. (See the chapter "Estate Planning" for more information regarding power of attorney.) You will need medical documentation and testimony to verify the need, and then you can be given this power either with or without your parent's consent.

If you have not talked about assuming power of attorney in advance, your parent may resist when it becomes necessary. It is unpleasant and difficult for an incompetent parent to give up his independence and control. The subject of power of attorney is best put on the table and thoroughly discussed when your parents are of sound mind and body.

You might say: "I saw this story in the newspaper the other day about siblings who were fighting in court over who should have control of the parents' financial accounts now that the parents were both older and apparently unable to make sound decisions. It made me wonder in what circumstances you would want to hand over power of attorney and who you would want to assign this power to. Have you thought about that?"

If you need to take power of attorney against your parent's wishes, it is good to do so as a united family. Gather together the support of your siblings and bring in your parent's siblings or close friends if you can. Performing such an intervention in alliance with other family members is a real asset when confronting and taking charge of an elderly parent's financial affairs. You should not have to do this alone.

If you don't have an extended family to help you, it can be best to have an objective third person be the one to announce that decision. You can ask the family doctor who documents your parent's incompetence to explain that, with your parent's best interest in mind, he or she must recommend that someone be given power of attorney over your parent's financial affairs.

Talking to our parents about how they manage their money is always a bit awkward and can seem intrusive. That's why it's best to make this a subject of general conversation long before there is a crisis situation that won't let you put off the dialogue any longer.

RESOURCES

American Association of Daily Money Managers (AADMM)
P.O. Box 755
Silver Spring, MD 20918
(301) 593-5462
www.aadmm.com

The AADMM can provide names of daily money managers in or near an older person's community. The association also publishes "Daily Money Management: What It Is and How Can It Help Me?"

Federal Deposit Insurance Corp. (FDIC)
801 Seventeenth Street NW
Washington, DC 20434
(800) 276-6003 or (202) 416-6940
www.fdic.gov

The FDIC publishes "Financial Caregiving: A Survival Guide"

EXPERT HELP

This chapter was written with the expert help of Robert O. Weagley, Ph.D., CPF, associate professor of consumer and family economics at the University of Missouri-Columbia. Dr. Weagley has published articles in *Financial Counseling and*

Planning, Journal of Consumer Affairs, and *Journal of Family and Economic Issues.* He is certified by the International Board of Standards and Practices of Certified Financial Planners. He is also a member of the American Council on Consumer Interests, the Academy of Financial Services, and the Association for Financial Counseling and Planning Education.

Consumer Fraud: Cons and Scams

We have to be willing to sit down and talk to our elderly parents about scams and cons because they happen all the time. Even though you think your parents could never be swindled, you need to know that these are slick professionals who are very good at finding an elderly person's vulnerable point and using it to make money. There are people out there who are looking to target the elderly every day.

Robert Scrivano, senior care planning consultant

It's not always easy to tell the difference between fraud and kindness. This is a question under investigation in the state of New Jersey, where a ninety-one-year-old widow changed her will shortly before her death, leaving a large chunk of her multimillion-dollar estate along with her ocean-view home to a forty-eight-year-old neighbor she had met eighteen months earlier. The challenge in this criminal investigation is to determine whether the woman changed her will freely, simply because she grew fond of her neighbor in her last months, or whether the neighbor took advantage of her in her weakest days and had one of his lawyers rewrite her will.

The verdict is still out on this case, but the situation points out a reality of life. All elderly people need to be especially leery of anyone who is suddenly interested in their well-being and their cares, wants, desires, and fears—whether this person calls on the phone, comes to the door, or is someone they meet at a social gathering or in their nursing home. Because the majority of consumer fraud crimes target senior citizens, this is a subject we should frequently talk about with our elderly parents.

This chapter shows you how to keep your parents safe from consumer fraud. It explains why this is a topic that can't be ignored and discusses the red flags to look for that indicate your parents are at risk for a rip-off. You'll also learn how to bring up the topic of fraud without embarrassing your parents and how to help them stay alert to both illegal and legal fraud schemes.

WHY TALK ABOUT FRAUD

There are many reasons why we should talk to our parents about the many faces of fraud, but the most pressing are these:

- People who are over sixty-five years old today hold the vast majority of the wealth in the United States.
- Many elderly people feel lonely. As a result of their isolation they are vulnerable to anyone who offers them a sympathetic ear, a little of their time, a sad story.
- The elderly come from a generation that was taught to be trusting and polite toward strangers. This makes them less likely to doubt a stranger's word, and they may find it difficult to hang up the phone or cut off a sales pitch.

- According to the National Consumers League, 27 percent of those who reported telemarketing fraud in 1999 were over the age of sixty. (Imagine how many more cases go unreported!)

Experts agree that when you put these facts together it's a recipe for trouble.

WHEN TO TALK ABOUT FRAUD

Jim watched with amusement as his mother seemed to bounce from one solicitor to the other at the shopping mall. "I thought it was funny the way they could zero in so quickly on an easy mark. She would stand there and answer their survey questions, try their free samples, and sign up for their giveaways and prizes. God bless her; she's so trusting and naive."

Jim was nearby to make sure his mother didn't get scammed into paying for something she didn't want, but what he found endearing—her being an easy mark—was really a red flag that should have alerted him to the need to talk to his mother about fraud. This was the perfect opportunity to bring up this subject and offer information and advice that would protect her finances the next time this happened and he wasn't around.

Like Jim's afternoon at the mall with his mom, there are certain times when a discussion about fraud with your parents would be especially helpful. This section looks at instances especially open to discussion:

- When there's a run of bogus (or even legit) mail or phone solicitations

- When something happens to force isolation
- When "travelers" come out
- When you see signs of early dementia

When There's a Run of Bogus (or Even Legit)
Mail or Phone Solicitations

Keep track of your own mail and telemarketing phone calls; if you receive announcements of contests, sweepstakes, and the like, talk to your parents about what you have received and why you would never support them.

This is a simple lesson Fran learned the hard way. She hung up the phone on the caller who announced her selection as the big prizewinner of a seven-day vacation for two—she knew this was too good to be true. She didn't think any more about it until her dad called the following week with the exciting news. He couldn't wait to tell her that he had just received a phone call from someone who said he had just won a free seven-day vacation for two at an island resort in the Caribbean. All he had to do was to give the prize coordinator his credit card number and checking account number to hold the plane and hotel reservations. He was told that within four weeks his tickets and reservations would arrive in the mail. He planned to surprise Fran's mom with the tickets for their anniversary. Wishing she had talked to her dad when she first received the same call, Fran suspected that the big surprise was going to be on him. Fran knew that giving out credit card and banking numbers over the phone is risky business. There are con artists out there who will take that information to run up large bills. Fran assumed that her dad knew this too but had lost sight of the danger in his hope of surprising and pleasing her mother.

When Something Happens to Force Isolation

The death of a spouse or friend, a move to a new geographical area, a close friend or family member's moving away—these are all events that can push our parents into isolation. This kind of occurrence makes the elderly more likely to be taken in by fraudulent schemes.

This was the case recently when an intelligent, newly widowed woman opened her door one day to find a girl in her late twenties begging for help. The girl told a heartbreaking story about the death of her young husband, the hunger of her two children, and the desperation that had driven her to go door-to-door in the hopes of finding a compassionate soul. The widow immediately went to her bank and withdrew $8,000 to hand to this young thief who had read the obituary in the paper and knew this elderly woman would be a prime target for her scam. The desire to feel needed and useful is often stronger than the person's sense of logic.

When "Travelers" Come Out

Travelers are seasonal scam artists who offer to do home repairs at a discount and then do shoddy work or none at all. Spring and summer are their busy seasons.

Seventy-five-year-old Ed knew all about these travelers, but when a young man knocked on his door one morning he fell for the pitch. "I just did a job up the street," the fellow said, "and I have some blacktop left over. I can do the job tomorrow morning and give you a real good price." Then came the catch: "I need half the money in cash now so I can pay my helper while I wait for the check from the last job to clear," he said. "If you can give me $200 right now, your driveway will be finished by tomorrow at noon." The young man looked honest enough, and the driveway really needed some work, so Ed handed over the money—and never saw the man again.

When You See Signs of Early Dementia

If your parent seems to be more forgetful lately or is having lapses in judgment or has recently made a decision that seems out of character, this is an indication that he is now also more vulnerable to being scammed.

Lou knew someone had taken advantage of his mother when he found ten cases of Florida fruit rotting in her basement. There was no way any honest salesperson would sell this much fruit to an elderly person living alone, but there it was.

WHAT YOU SHOULD TALK ABOUT

It's a good idea to talk to your parents about how they can recognize rip-offs and how they can protect themselves from both legal and illegal fraud. You need to remind them, "There are people out there who don't have your best interest at heart and will lie to you and steal from you."

Breaking the Ice

To keep up on the potentially fraudulent situations your parents may be encountering, it's also important to talk with them about the weather at least once a week. This may sound like odd advice, but when you make casual conversation you'll find out who they've been talking to this week, who wanted to make an appointment to come over and talk about finances, or who came to their door selling things. You can gather much of the information you need to protect your parents from con artists through conversations rather than inquisitions.

It's also important to let your parents know that if they should get scammed, they shouldn't feel too embarrassed to tell you about it. A sense of embarrassment kept Janet's mother from telling her that she had given a check to a guy who rang her doorbell one morning offering to paint her house for a very reasonable price of $2,000. This smooth talker convinced Janet's mom that he needed the money up front to buy the paint. Just like teenagers who feel they "can't" tell their parents about the mess they're in and then end up in even deeper trouble, elderly parents like Janet's who "can't" tell their children about a lapse in judgment are likely to lose the opportunity for restitution.

You might say: "If you ever make a bad deal or feel you've been swindled, let me know right away. I might be able to help you get your money back. You can cancel the check, call the credit card company, or even call the police. Call me as soon as you think you may have made a mistake."

Addressing Specific Issues
Consumer fraud comes in two varieties, and you should talk to your parents about both kinds:

1. The obviously illegal kind that breaks the law when people are scammed
2. The perfectly legal kind, such as selling ten cases of grapefruit to an elderly person

Talk About Illegal Fraud.   Customs agents describe a recently popular scam that involves a phone call and a winning lottery number. The scam artist, claiming to be a customs agent on the telephone, asks the senior citizen to verify his or her identity, Social Security number, and a credit card number because the scam artist is holding a $50,000 cashier's check from a lottery in England. But in order for the person to receive the $50,000 cashier's check, the senior citizen needs to send a cashier's check for $3,000 to a certain individual to pay the English tax on the money and to avoid any problems with the U.S. Internal Revenue Service. The next day, the senior citizen receives a call from another person identifying himself as an FBI agent who is calling to verify the credibility of the first caller who needed the personal information. This usually seals the deal, and the senior citizen is soon scammed out of $3,000 and is the victim of identity theft.

Other illegal senior citizen scams come in the mail. Recently, bogus letters were mailed to elderly black people across the South telling them they might be eligible for $5,000 reimbursements. One letter stated that the federal government was seeking individuals entitled to payments under a supposed "Slave Reparation Act." And another alerted recipients that they were due $5,000 because of a glitch in the Social Security collection process. Both letters, which were sent by mail and also circulated in churches and senior centers, instructed people to submit their name, address, telephone number, and Social Security number to the "National Victims Registrar" in Washington and expect payments to be added to future government benefits checks or issued in a lump sum. These letters were nothing more than a scam aimed at stealing people's identities and running up credit bills under their names.

It's well known that the elderly are often targets of illegal scams. They are prey for the traveling con artists we've talked about who break the law by offering a low price for maintenance or home repairs and then doing shoddy work or completely disappearing. Senior citizens also fall victim to shady telemarketers who offer bogus prizes, phony travel packages, get-rich-quick investments, and fake charities. To protect your parents from this kind of swindle, you should talk about these kinds of stories. Give them a straightforward word of warning—without being pushy.

You might say: "I don't want to interfere in your lives, but I have heard about some very common and unscrupulous scams I thought you should know about so you don't get taken for a ride."

You can also try to make sure they understand the basic rules of consumer safety.

You might say: "I think it's a good idea to meet several times with any agent who's selling something. Experts say you should never turn over any money the first time you meet a vendor."

You might say: "When I was looking for someone to replace my kitchen cabinets last year, I found out that it's smart to call several companies for bids and estimates and advice. Before you hire anybody to work for you, try to go to at least three different sources. This gives you a better chance of finding an honest person who might say, 'You really don't need this at all.'"

You might say: "If you're ever in doubt or if a deal seems too good to be true, you can always ask your attorney [or CPA, or both] for their opinion of the purchase before you hand over any money."

You should also talk about specific red flags that should alert your parents to a possible scam.

You might say: "I was reading this booklet about consumer fraud, and it gave some tips about how to avoid getting taken. It said to suspect offers that say you must act now or the offer will expire, or that say you've won a free gift, vacation, or prize but you must pay for some other charge like postage or handling, or that say you must send money, give a credit card or bank account number, or have your check picked up by courier for immediate payment."

Frequently ask your parents: "Have you noticed any of these kinds of come-ons?"

You can also help your parents get over their reluctance to seem impolite when they want to end an unwanted sales phone call. Give them a few easy phrases they can say, such as the following:

"I don't do business with people I don't know."
"I need to see written information about your offer before I consider giving you money."
"You can send that information to my attorney's office."
"Please put me on your Do-Not-Call list."
"I'm not interested. Thank you and good-bye."

Talk About Legal Fraud.   Even elderly parents who would be very cautious and savvy about handing over their money to a con artist can be easily taken in by a person in a business suit working for a legitimate firm. That's why the elderly are prime clients for unscrupulous businesspeople who commit "legal fraud" by taking advantage of the vulnerabilities of the elderly and using their fear of nursing homes, for example, to manipulate them into buying financial products they don't need. The elderly are bilked out of millions of dollars each year in this manner through the sale of unnecessary life insurance polices, annuities, and long-term care insurance. Your parents should never be skimping on food or housing payments to pay for things like long-term care insurance. If, for example, $700 of a person's monthly income of $2,000 is going out for any kind of insurance policy, something is very wrong.

An unhappy son tells the story of his elderly mother who owned a $400,000 home and was about to move into an assisted living home. A financial investor (who was also a real estate agent) convinced her that if she did not sell the house and put the money into an annuity she would lose everything to the state. What he did not tell her was that these transactions would give him $65,000 in commissions and that the true circumstances were that the state would not take any money and that her financial arrangements had nothing to do with Medicaid or MediCal. Fortunately, her son put a stop to the deal when his mother's neighbor called to tell him that there was a For Sale sign on the house.

In another case, an elderly man bought a $65,000 life insurance policy because the agent played on his fear of leaving his wife alone and destitute. He paid a $60,000 premium for this peace of mind! The agent played on his most intimate fears and convinced him that this was a sound decision. This is shameful and deceptive, but it is legal.

It's best to let your parents know that you want to be with them whenever they meet with salespeople.

You might say: "There are so many ways that a slick salesperson can give you a bad deal that I sometimes get confused trying to keep track of all the details of our agreement; I know it helps having my wife [husband] with me to catch what I don't. I'd like to help you the same way. When you're going to meet with any kind of salesperson, let me know, and I'll come with you."

If you think your parents might be offended if you say you want to be in the room when they keep a sales appointment, try a different tactic.

You might say: "You know, I'm interested in finding out about that for myself also. Can I sit in on your meeting to hear what the person has to say?"

If you fear your parents are not as mentally sharp as they used to be and worry that they are easy prey, you should be more direct. First tell them an anecdotal story about an educated person who was swindled out of a load of money, then get to the point.

You might say: "This could happen to anyone. I'd like you to promise me that you'll tell me about any deals you want to get involved in before you sign a contract or hand over any money."

Fortunately, there are laws to protect the elderly against consumer fraud, and there are organizations and agencies such as those listed in the Resources to keep track of unscrupulous vendors and offer advice and protection. Nevertheless, your parents, by virtue of their age, are prime targets for fraud; it's a good idea to talk about this reality and offer your help and support.

RESOURCES

Consumer Response Center (CRC)
Federal Trade Commission
Washington, DC 20580
(202) FTC-HELP (382-4357)
www.ftc.gov

You can file a complaint with the commission by contacting the CRC by phone, mail, or e-mail; you can also use the complaint form on the website.

National Consumers League
1701 K Street NW
Washington, DC 20006
(202) 835-3323
www.natlconsumersleague.org

The National Consumers League and AARP conducted research on telemarketing fraud targeting the elderly; they offer suggestions for older people and their families in a brochure called "They Can't Hang Up," available from the National Consumers League.

To stop telephone sales calls from many legitimate national marketers, send your name, address, and telephone number to:
Direct Marketing Association
Telephone Preference Service
P.O. Box 9014
Farmingdale, NY 11735

To remove your name from many national direct mail lists, write to:
Direct Marketing Association
Mail Preference Service
P.O. Box 9008
Farmingdale, NY 11735

If you suspect a telephone scam, call your state attorney general. The Federal Trade Commission's Telemarketing Sales Rule gives state law enforcement officers the power to prosecute fraudulent telemarketers.

EXPERT HELP

This chapter was written with the expert help of Robert Scrivano, senior care planning consultant. Based in Sacramento, California, Scrivano has more than twenty-two years of experience as an independent senior care planning consultant. He has saved numerous senior citizens from financial ruin by debunking the misleading and false information circulating about senior financial issues and exposing complex fraud schemes and scams aimed at the elderly. Scrivano currently sits on the district attorney's commission on elder financial abuse.

Long-Term Care Insurance

Long-term care insurance is a good solution to the problems that are part of being in the "sandwich generation." It lets elderly parents keep control of their assets and their financial independence, and it frees the children from being in a position where they must physically care for or plan for an elder parent's disability.

David Bendix, CPA/PFS, CFP, CFS, RFC

Al's dad worked full-time until the age of seventy-two. Al described him as a "workhorse" who was never sick a day in his life. Because his dad had always been active and had many interests and hobbies, Al expected that he would enjoy a robust retirement.

Two years into his long-awaited retirement, Al's dad had a stroke that left him completely paralyzed on his right side. He needed constant care, physical rehabilitation, occupational therapy, and a great deal of medical attention. As Al was weighing the options of nursing homes, assisted living homes, and in-home care, he couldn't help worrying about the cost. He knew his dad needed and deserved good medical attention, but how on earth would he pay for it?

219

Thousands of adult children throughout the country face this dilemma each day. We want the best for our aging, possibly ill parents, but this care is expensive. Long-term care is quite different from the acute care given in hospitals to help a person get better. Acute care lasts for only a short time, and most of our parents have medical coverage to pay the cost. Long-term care, in contrast, is provided to people with chronic, degenerative illness or disabilities who require continued support over a long period of time; such care is not covered under most medical policies. These services can include the following:

- Help in the person's home with daily activities like bathing and dressing
- Community programs, such as adult day care
- Assisted living services, such as meals, health monitoring, and help with daily activities—provided in a special residential setting other than the person's home
- Care in a nursing home

This chapter discusses why long-term care insurance is so necessary today. It suggests when to bring up the subject and how to work the topic into discussions without sounding controlling or nosy. It helps you talk about government programs, choosing an insurance agent, mapping out the details, and available sources and options. Putting this subject on the table can save your parents (and you) from financial ruin as they age and need more and more care.

WHY TALK ABOUT LONG-TERM CARE INSURANCE

Rising life expectancy rates mean that many of our parents will live well into their eighties and nineties. This is good news, of course, but a study by the U.S. Department of Health and Human Services projects that people ages sixty-five and older face a 43 percent risk of needing nursing home care at some time in their lives. Add to this the fact that 80 percent of U.S. women live a portion of their adult lives alone, either by choice or because of widowhood or divorce, and the need for long-term care protection becomes evident. Because many of our parents will need some kind of care for their mental or physical health, long-term care insurance is a financial issue we need to talk about.

We should talk to our parents about long-term care insurance because the financial consequences of avoiding the subject can be devastating, and too many families find this out the hard way. After Charlotte put her mother, Lillian, in a nearby nursing home, she sat at home dazed by the mere thought of finding the approximately $60,000 a year she would need to allow her mother to stay there. She thought about bringing her mother into her own home and arranging for home care, but she knew that such care also can be very costly: an older person who receives just three home health visits per week could pay about $12,000 for home care each year. Those with severe impairments will pay even more, as will those who have no one nearby to help them. Although invaluable and necessary, this care can diminish a person's assets and cause great financial difficulties in the future.

This is exactly what ultimately happened to Charlotte's mother. When Lillian had her first major stroke, she needed full-time care in a nursing home. First she drew on her savings account to pay the bills. Then she cashed in her company stocks. Then she sold off her prized antiques. Finally she sold her home. When all this money was spent four years later, Lillian became eligible for Medicaid, but this coverage did not allow her to stay in the nursing facility that had become her home. She was required to transfer to a different nursing home, which was much further away from Charlotte and her family. The move was a terrible blow for Lillian, who had made many dear friends at the first nursing home and looked forward to frequent visits from her daughter.

Charlotte, her husband, and her children were also deeply affected by all that was happening to Lillian. They felt heartbroken as they watched her lose all her money, possessions, and assets that she had worked so hard all her life to accumulate. And they were also were extremely distressed over what Lillian's financial problems were doing to their own plans. Charlotte's mother had long promised her collection of valuable antiques and her home to Charlotte. She and her husband had counted on these things to feed their retirement. Now, not only did they lose these assets, but their savings account was being drained because they felt responsible for paying the cost of Lillian's care that was not covered by Medicaid. This worry trickled down to Charlotte's children, who were concerned that their parents would no longer be financially fit for retirement and would need their support. Lillian would have been crushed if she had known how the high cost of her care was affecting her daughter's family.

Although it's difficult for our parents (or anyone for that matter) to imagine themselves in need of expensive long-term care, it's worth the effort to talk about the kind of insurance that would cover this potential financial drain. Ultimately, if your parents need long-term care, become incapacitated either mentally or physically, or both, you (and any siblings) will become responsible for their care. Because you will be involved at that point (whether you really want to be or not), it's important to talk to your parents now so that you can later make decisions that address their expressed wishes and needs.

WHEN TO TALK ABOUT LONG-TERM CARE INSURANCE

When the doctor told Steve that his mother was in the very early stages of Alzheimer's disease, he was quite naturally very upset and worried about her future health. But he was also worried about the high cost of the long-term assisted living or nursing home care she would probably need. He called his insurance agent to get the details on long-term care insurance, hoping this would be the answer, but the news wasn't good. Because his mother was over seventy-two years old, the cost made long-term care insurance no longer a viable option. When the insured person is this age the premiums are extremely high, and as each year passes they become more and more unaffordable.

To avoid a situation like this, it's important to talk about long-term care insurance long before it's needed and while your parents are of sound mind. Generally it is available only to those who are in relatively good health physically and mentally. Ideally it's best to talk to your parents about this subject when they are still middle aged (when they can get the best terms and when the rates are lowest). However, the unfortunate reality of this situation is that most families do not start thinking about long-term care insurance until the parents are sixty to seventy years of age. Whatever your parents' ages, if you haven't done so already, the best time to talk to them about this issue is right now.

WHAT YOU SHOULD TALK ABOUT

It is always touchy to talk about family money, so rather than tell your parents that they must buy this kind of insurance, you should make an effort to get them to think about what is best for them. Conversations about long-term care insurance should involve a give-and-take of information. You can use a few conversation strategies that break the ice before you move into the details of long-term care insurance.

Breaking the Ice

It may seem that there is just no easy way to ease into saying something like, "So Mom, how do you plan to pay for nursing home care if you ever need it?" It certainly can be very awkward to bring up the subject of long-term care insurance, because when you ask your parents how they plan to pay for any long-term care they may need when they get older, you risk sounding as though you want to make sure it's not going to cost *you* anything.

When you discuss this important subject, you can break the ice and reduce misunderstandings if you talk about

- Other people who need long-term care
- Your concerns about paying for your own long-term care
- What-if situations

Talk About Other People Who Need Long-Term Care. A conversation about long-term care is easier to get into if someone you know has gone through the experience. You can use their situation as a springboard for discussion. When Brad's mom casually mentioned that she had mailed a card to her sister at the nursing home just to say hello, Brad used that opening to broach the subject of cost and planning. He said, "I've heard that long-term care can be very expensive. Do you know how Aunt Mary's family manages the cost?" This kind of third-person look at the cost of long-term care will help your parent start thinking about the cost of care and how others manage it.

You might say: "Dad, my friend's dad is getting older and needs daily care. After a lot of thought and discussion, he and his family think that he would do well in one of those assisted living facilities. But they've now found out that they are very expensive, and the father doesn't have long-term care insurance. In fact, they didn't know that that kind of policy even existed to pay for things like home care or community care centers, nursing homes, or assisted living services. Have you ever heard about long-term care insurance?"

Talking about other people your parents know who need long-term care also removes the obstacle of "this will never happen to me" that makes discussion difficult. Their knowing someone who is in need of long-term care makes it easier to acknowledge the possibility and increases their willingness to plan for it.

You might say: "Your friend Betsy was always so healthy. Who would have thought she would have to sell her house to pay for nursing home care? That must have broken her heart; I know she would have liked to leave the house to her son. I'd hate to see something like that happen to you. Do you have the kind of insurance that helps pay for long-term care? Would you like me to get you some information about how you can protect your assets if you need long-term care at any point?"

Talk About Your Concerns About Paying for Your Own Long-Term Care. If you haven't already, you might look into a long-term care policy for yourself and discuss your findings with your parents in conversation. Tell them that you've been thinking about how financially disruptive it can be to need long-term care, and you want to make sure that you're covered. (Someone like actor Christopher Reeve reminds us all that the need for long-term medical care could happen to anyone at any time.)

You might say: "I recently heard about a type of insurance that would pay the bills if I ever needed long-term care in a rehabilitation center or even a nursing home when I'm older. I think I'd like to get this and protect my assets. "Do you know anything about long-term care insurance? Do you have a long-term care policy, or have you thought about one?"

Talk About What-If Situations.   The what-if questioning technique can help you ease the subject of long-term care insurance into the conversation. After talking about someone you know or someone in the news (or someone you make up!) who needs long-term care, ask your parents these what-if questions:

"What if that happened to you? Could you afford good care?"
"What if you have to eventually go into a nursing home; do you have the kind of insurance that would cover the cost?"
"What if you became very sick and needed long-term care? Have you thought about how you want to protect yourself financially?"

There are a lot of what-if questions you can ask when talking about others or about your own parents specifically so as to open up the subject of long-term care insurance.

Breaking the ice on this subject allows for a two-way dialogue rather than a mandate: "You have to buy long-term care insurance."

Addressing Specific Issues

The subject of long-term care insurance has many issues attached. After you broach the subject in general, you'll need to keep the conversation alive to delve into such details as these:

- The difference between Medicaid and long-term care insurance
- Where to get long-term care insurance
- How to find a good insurance agent
- How to select an insurance company
- Choosing coverage carefully

Talk About the Difference Between Medicaid and Long-Term Care Insurance.   Talk about which government programs you can count on and which ones you can't. Many seniors believe that Medicare will pay for the custodial care of a long-term illness—but it will not. It will cover some care for a short while, but it is not intended for ongoing care. Medicaid too is not the resource many think it is. This is a form of aid that can be tapped into as a measure of last resort only when all other assets are gone.

You might say: "Mom, I saw this TV show the other night about Medicare and Medicaid. I was surprised to find out that Medicaid would not pay for most long-term care needs of the elderly until they have exhausted their own assets. They also said that using Medicaid for long-term care can limit your choice of nursing homes. They talked about something called long-term care insurance that you can buy to protect your assets and make sure you get the care you may need. Have you ever heard of this kind of insurance? I thought it sounded like something you might be interested in."

Talk About Where to Get Long-Term Care Insurance. Today
many corporations offer an insurance package that includes long-
term care insurance. If your parents are still working, they may be
eligible to buy this insurance through their employer. If they are
retired, they have two options, and you should talk to them about
the advantages and disadvantages of each:

1. They can buy this insurance through various senior associations, such as the American Association of Retired Persons
   (AARP) or a union group that offers these benefits to members.
2. They can buy their own policy from a private insurance
   company.

*Talk About the Advantages and Disadvantages of Association-
Related Long-Term Care Insurance.* The advantage of coverage
offered through a large association is that the underwriting is more
lenient. The likelihood of getting approval to take out a policy is
greater for elderly people—even those with some type of preexisting condition.

The disadvantage of this kind of plan is twofold: first, this large
pool of people who were given coverage under lenient conditions
may strain the financial health of the association by making many
claims in the same period of time. This makes the members subject
to periodic rate adjustments.

The second disadvantage of an association-related long-term
care policy is that it offers only blanket coverage. Association policies assign nonnegotiable benefits and coverage that you cannot
change to fit your personal needs. If you'd like $200-per-day bene-
fits but the plan offers only $100-per-day coverage, you cannot have
what you want.

You might say: "Mom, you've been retired from teaching only two years now. Why don't you call the teacher's union to find out if they offer some kind of long-term care insurance and if you're still eligible to buy a policy?"

You might say: "I know your insurance agent told you that you are not eligible to buy long-term care insurance, but I'll bet that if you looked into policies offered through a group like AARP you might find something. Here's their phone number; why not give them a call?"

Talk About the Advantages and Disadvantages of Buying Long-Term Care Insurance from Private Companies. If your parents go to a private insurance carrier, they will find that this type of service also offers advantages and disadvantages. Having their own insurance agent write a policy is very desirable because it allows them to dictate the kind of coverage they want. For example, they can decide if they want the policy to cover hospice care or home health care. They can choose the period of time for which they want coverage and choose the deductible best for them. At first glance, this sounds like the best way to get long-term care coverage, but choosing private carriers to underwrite the policy can also have its drawbacks.

Trying to buy a policy from a private carrier can be difficult for the elderly, because carriers who write policies for individuals instead of large groups are more restrictive in their choice of applicants. They tend to insure younger, healthier people as a way to lower their risk of needing to make periodic rate adjustments to handle a high volume of claims. This was good news for Taylor's dad, who was a relatively young sixty-six years old and had no health problems. This was bad news for Nick's dad, who could not find a private carrier to insure him because he was a relatively old seventy-five years old and had had a small stroke several years ago.

You might say: "Mom, why don't you try to get a long-term care policy from a private carrier first? If this doesn't work, I'll help you look for one through an association catering to senior citizens."

Talk About How to Find a Good Insurance Agent.   Long-term care insurance policies are complicated. If your parents choose to buy coverage from a private carrier, they will find themselves wading through mounds of details trying to get the right coverage in terms of deductibles, benefit periods, the waiting period, inflation riders, and nursing home care versus home care coverage. They need someone who knows their stuff.

You might say: "It's important to find an insurance agent who has experience with long-term care policies. Although the agent who carries your home and car insurance may be a good friend, the details of long-term care can be quite complicated, and you should have someone who knows what you need. An agent who sells life or health insurance or one who specializes in long-term care policies is best for this kind of coverage."

Choose the agent carefully. There are many unscrupulous people out there looking to prey on the elderly's fear of nursing homes and of financial disaster. Ask a trusted financial adviser, attorney, or family friend for a personal referral.

Talk About How to Select an Insurance Company.   You should be sure to research the background of the company offering long-term care insurance. It's important to choose a reputable company that is likely to be in business when you need the benefits.

You might say: "Before you sign any policy, Mom and Dad, why don't you check out the company to make sure it's going to be able to deliver when you need it? Find out how long it has been in business and how long it has offered this kind of policy. I'll help you check with the Better Business Bureau to see if there have been any complaints filed against this firm."

Talk About Choosing Coverage Carefully. The cost of a long-term care insurance policy depends on the coverage you choose. There are many details your parents should be on the lookout for before they sign.

You might say: "Here's a list of questions that insurance experts suggest you ask before you buy a long-term care policy. Why don't you discuss them with your agent before you sign?"

Are there any conditions that you must meet to collect the benefits?

Will the policy pay for home care or hospice care? Under what conditions?

Does the policy cover home health care?

Does the policy cover preexisting conditions?

Can you increase the benefit amount over time to keep up with inflation?

What are the deductible periods?

What benefit periods are available (two-year, three-year, four-year, or lifetime)?

You don't need to be an expert on long-term care insurance to talk about this subject with your parents. After you break the ice and go over the basics, you can refer your parents to an insurance agent who can give them all the details. You might even set up the appointment and accompany them. You can also learn more about long-term coverage through the Resources listed here.

RESOURCES

Insurance Counseling and Assistance (ICA) provides free help with questions about long-term care costs. If you are confused about Medicare coverage of nursing home services, Medicaid eligibility requirements, or private long-term care insurance, or if you have health insurance questions, contact your state's area agency on aging and ask for a referral to your local ICA program.

National Association of Insurance Commissioners (NAIC)
2301 McGee
Suite 800
Kansas City, MO 64108
(816) 842-3600
www.naic.org

The NAIC publishes "A Shopper's Guide to Long-Term Care Insurance," which contains information on all aspects of long-term care insurance and the addresses and telephone numbers for every state insurance department, agency on aging, and insurance counseling program.

United Seniors Health Cooperative (USHC)
409 Third Street SW, 2nd floor
Washington, DC 20024
(800) 637-2604
www.unitedseniorshealth.org

The USHC publishes *Long-Term Care Planning: A Dollar and Sense Guide*, which is available for $19.50 through their website.

AARP publishes a booklet called "Before You Buy—A Guide to Long-Term Care Insurance." To request a free copy (ask for document no. D12893), write to:
AARP Fulfillment
601 E Street NW
Washington, DC 20049
www.aarp.org/caregive/2-ltcf.htm

Health Care Financing Administration (HCFA)
www.hcfa.gov

The HCFA maintains an Internet website that provides information about paying for long-term care. Visit the website to access the Health Insurance Counseling Program, which provides free volunteer counseling on Medicare, managed care, and private insurance in all states.

Insurance News Network (INN)
This independent, consumer-friendly website provides free and unbiased information useful in understanding and choosing insurance policies. Most helpful are its rate comparisons and tools for evaluating insurance policies. But it also has ratings of insurance companies, industry news, and guidance on how to file a complaint.
http://www.insure.com

EXPERT HELP

This chapter was written with the expert help of David Bendix, CPA/PFS, CFP, CFS, RFC. Bendix is president and founder of the Bendix Financial Group in Garden City, New York. He is a certified public accountant who has obtained the personal financial specialist designation from the American Institute of Certified Public Accountants (AICPA) and is a certified financial planner. He is also a certified fund specialist and registered financial consultant. Bendix is a registered securities principal affiliated with Royal Alliance Associates Inc. (a member firm of the National Association of Securities Dealers). He is also a registered investment adviser through the Bendix Financial Group, Inc., and an independently licensed life and health insurance agent. You can access Bendix's website at www.BendixFinancial.com to obtain additional information on long-term care.

Estate Planning

It's true that talking to a parent about estate planning can make an adult child appear to be greedy, but making sure that the parents' wishes are carried out after death is not a selfish thing to do.

Gary Katz, wealth preservation planning specialist
with Sagemark Consulting, a division of the
Lincoln Financial Group in New Jersey

Long before Jack and Betty died together in an automobile accident, they sat down and talked to their four children about their will. They owned a car dealership worth $5 million and wanted to leave the business to the two sons who worked there. They left their other assets, also valued at approximately $5 million, to their two daughters. This seemed fair and equitable to everyone, so with hugs and wishes for a long, healthy life, the family felt secure in this plan. However, what they did not know was that the taxes on the estate would be taken from the girls' share of the assets. In the end, the sons got the business and the daughters got nothing. This was not what the parents wanted, of course, but without careful estate planning, this is what can happen.

Talking about their parents' money, investments, and property and their beneficiary designations from retirement plans, life insurance, and annuities is not easy for many adult children. Some think, "What they do with their assets is their own business." Others may say, "How can I tell them what to do to make sure I get all the money I think is coming to me?" Yet if you don't talk about this subject, your parents may die thinking they have provided well for you and your family when in fact they handed you the complex, expensive, and time-consuming job of trying to hold on to at least some of the inheritance they wanted you to have.

This chapter introduces you to estate planning so that you can decide if this is a subject you should talk to your parents about. But remember, this is a very general overview of a complex subject. The topics explained here give you an idea of the kinds of information your parents should investigate with a professional estate planner. The information is not intended to help you set up an estate plan; it is intended to show you a variety of reasons why talking to your parents about this subject and getting them to talk to a professional estate planner can be a good idea.

WHY TALK ABOUT ESTATE PLANNING

There are lots of reasons to talk about estate planning. Some adult children may not like the way their parents decide to will their assets. They may feel Dad's second wife shouldn't inherit the family business. They may feel their parents are too generous to charity or old Aunt Tilly. They may feel that distant sibling Bobby shouldn't get the same amount as they who have been taking care of Mom day in and day out for years. In these cases, the adult children have very personal reasons to talk to their parents.

However, these personal reasons are not the focus of this chapter. This chapter explores the situation in which you are not trying to change your parents' desires or intentions but rather are wanting to help your parents reach three important estate planning goals:

1. To avoid unnecessary probate problems
2. To avoid losing an excessive amount of the estate to taxes
3. To make sure that your parents' wishes are carried out

To Avoid Unnecessary Probate Problems

Estate planning can control how much of your parents' estate will go through legal probate. Probate, simply stated, is the administration of a person's estate by the court. Even when there is a valid will, probate can be time-consuming and, in some states, very costly and complicated. The average cost of probate ranges from 3 to 10 percent of the gross estate. The amount of time for the probate process to be completed can be anywhere from eighteen months to two years or even three or four years! In addition, probate is a very public affair. If your parent plans to leave a family business to heirs, probate may expose business records to competitors and creditors as well. Avoiding probate is one way to protect one's privacy.

To Avoid Losing an Excessive Amount of the Estate to Taxes

Estate planning can protect assets from taxation. If your mom has assets of $3 million, the tax on this money after her death is $1 million. That's a lot of hard-earned cash being handed over to the government, cash that the parent thought would be going to her heirs.

To Make Sure That Your Parents' Wishes Are Carried Out

Failing to plan carefully for the distribution of the family assets can have unintended consequences. For example, Hernando owned a trucking business and had three sons. In his will he left the business to all three, thinking this was fair and equitable. However, after Hernando's death, the eldest son, who was the only one working in the business, suddenly became the minority shareholder. With two-thirds of the business in their possession, the two younger brothers voted the eldest out and brought in a professional management company to run the business. Hernando did not plan for that possibility, and there was nothing the elder son could do about it.

You should talk to your parents about estate planning so they can decide how much of their estate will go to family, friends, and institutions of choice and how much will go to taxes and attorneys.

WHEN TO TALK ABOUT ESTATE PLANNING

When seventy-six-year-old widowed Jerry married Catherine, his son was very happy for him. "My dad had been alone for so long," says Kurt, "and I thought his marriage to Catherine was a real blessing for him. I couldn't have been happier at that time." But what Kurt didn't know was that after his marriage, Jerry changed his will, leaving all his assets to his new wife. "I'm sure my dad wanted to be sure she would be secure and cared for in her old age," reasons Kurt, "but I'm also sure he didn't intend things to work out the way they have." When Jerry died a few years later, his estate was turned over to Catherine as he had requested. Later, upon her death, Catherine left that estate to her five children from a previous marriage. Kurt was disinherited. Of course he can legally contest the will, but he is sure that his father never intended that he would have to engage in a long, expensive court battle to share in his inheritance.

Kurt's story highlights why it is so important to talk about estate planning at the time of major life events. Such events as retirement, birth of grandchildren, death of a spouse, divorce, and remarriage all call for a closer look at or reassessment of how a person's assets will be distributed. These events give you a good opportunity to bring up the subject with your parents. (Be sure to tell them that they cannot makes changes to a will simply by crossing out one directive and writing in another. All changes must be made with what's called a legal codicil.)

Knowing the right time to talk about estate planning still doesn't make talking easy. Estate planning is a part of death planning, so it automatically becomes something that many families don't want to talk about—ever. "How can I talk about my parents' will?" some adult children ask. "It will sound like I'm putting them in an early grave. They're in great health; I can't bring up the subject of their death." This is an understandable line of reasoning, but the fact is, while they're in good health is the only time you can talk about estate planning. The law requires that a person making a will must possess sufficient mental capacity to understand the extent of property owned, as well as the effect of a will in disposing of such property. If you wait until you see signs of dementia or severe physical illness to urge your parents to "get their affairs in order," it will be too late.

WHAT YOU SHOULD TALK ABOUT

The details of estate planning are many and complex. Unless you have background in this area of law and taxation, you should not try to tell your parents how to manage their assets. However, you can introduce them to the idea of estate planning and guide them in the right direction.

Breaking the Ice

Because talking about money—especially money that may be given to you upon the death of your parents—can be awkward, you may want to break the ice on this topic by easing into the conversation indirectly. You can do this by talking about

- Other people and their estate circumstances and problems
- Your own experiences with estate planning
- General facts that make for good dinner-table discussions

Talk About Other People's Experiences. To get your parents thinking about the different aspects of estate planning, tell them about the experiences of your friends or your friends' parents. You can even use any of the anecdotes in this chapter to get them thinking about the subject.

You might say: "Dad, listen to this. I was just talking to my friend Jenny, and she was so upset. It seems that Jenny's mother, who was a pretty wealthy widow, died recently and left Jenny her house and quite a bit of stock investments. Well, it turns out that the taxes on these things were so high that Jenny now has to sell either the house or the stocks to pay the taxes. What a shame. Jenny says that if her mother had talked to an estate planner before her death this wouldn't have happened. Have you ever talked to an estate planner?"

Talk About Your Own Experiences with Estate Planning. If you yourself have reason to worry about the way your assets will be distributed to your heirs, see an estate planner and tell your parents what you learn. This will get them thinking about their own affairs.

If you don't yet have enough assets to warrant estate planning, you still might begin talking about yourself and then turn the discussion around to them.

You might say: "A coworker of mine is married to an estate planner. He was saying that if my assets are over $675,000 I should definitely use an estate planner to protect them from excessive taxation after my death. Well, I'm not ready for that yet, but it did make me wonder if you've ever thought about using a trust to keep your assets from being heavily taxed and brought through probate after your death."

Talk About General Facts. If your family openly talks about current events or the latest financial news, you can introduce the subject of estate planning into any of these conversations. There is often news on this subject after the death of a wealthy celebrity or when family members contest a will. You can objectively talk about the facts of estate planning with the easy-to-use phrase "Did you know that . . . ?"

You might say: "Did you know that when the legendary newspaper magnate William Randolph Hearst died at the age of eighty-eight he didn't leave any of his five sons in charge of his empire? The holdings were handed over to professional managers, and the sons became the minority on a thirteen-member board of trustees. I wonder if he did that on purpose or if he just assumed his sons would have the right to inherit his business? Estate planning is a very complex thing. Have you ever talked to an estate planner about your assets?"

You might say: "Mom and Dad, a friend of mine just told me that a will that is valid in one state is often not valid in another. Did you know that? Have you had an attorney in California review your will since you moved there?"

You might say: "Did you know that if you don't do careful estate planning, 70 percent of your IRA may go to the government in taxes?"

You might say: "Did you know that you can buy insurance to pay the taxes on your estate when you die?

Addressing Specific Issues

There are far too many specific issues involved in estate planning to talk in detail on this subject with your parents, but you can give them this outline of the basics and then help them find an experienced estate planner who can fill in the gaps. The following are a few topics you might want to discuss:

- Four ways to pass assets to heirs
- Estate tax reduction strategies
- Power of attorney
- Finding an estate planner

Talk About Four Ways to Pass Assets to Heirs. The basics about the transfer of assets after death come down to the fact that there are four ways to pass assets to heirs:

Intestate Succession. Joe was a well-respected, wealthy businessman. His intellect and professionalism impressed all who knew him. He worked hard all his life and had carefully made investments over the years that he knew would keep him and his wife comfortable during their retirement. He had purchased three income-producing properties that he often mentioned he planned to pass on to his three children. Then Joe died unexpectedly of a heart attack at the age of sixty-eight, and everyone in his family was shocked to find that he did not have a will. After a lengthy (not to mention costly) probate process, Joe's assets were not distributed as his family knew he had intended. The court was free to determine who would receive what and when.

If your parent dies without a will, the same thing will happen to her estate. Like Joe's, it will pass to her heirs under the intestate succession laws of her state, with no guarantee that the property will be distributed to the desired heirs. All nearest relatives get a piece of the estate, but no one else does—and no one gets more than the state-allotted share, even if it's unfair. Stepchildren usually get nothing. This approach leaves the distribution of assets open to protest. The family might battle with the courts. A fight might break out among your relatives over who runs the inheritance. Obviously, this is not a desirable situation.

An intestate succession plan is easiest for the living parent— he or she does nothing, and it costs nothing. But it can be costly to the heirs in terms of expense and distribution to the wrong people. Make sure your parents know that writing a will is key to ensuring that the people to whom they want to leave their property actually get it.

You might say: "Mom, do you have a legal will drawn up? It's not that I expect you'll be needing it any time soon, but I was just reading that if you don't have a will your wishes may not be carried out, because the state will decide who gets what. I knew you wouldn't like things handled that way, so I just want to make sure you have a valid will."

Joint Tenancy. Joint tenancy is a method of holding title to assets. Your mother and father may have the deed to their home in a joint tenancy. This means that when one dies, the other automatically is heir to the home without going through the probate process. In this case, joint tenancy makes sense. However, joint tenancy is generally not a good idea between anyone except spouses.

If your mother wants you to have her house upon her death, it might seem that joint tenancy would make sense. This arrangement takes precedence over a will and avoids probate upon the death of your parent. But being a joint tenant opens both you and your parent to possible financial difficulties that you should be aware of:

- Suppose you share joint tenancy with your mother on her home and bank account. Someone trips on the crooked sidewalk leading up to your house and breaks a hip. This person sues you for neglect and wins a sizable judgment against you. Because you are a joint tenant of your mother's home and bank account, each can be considered as part of your estate. You could lose your share as part of a legal judgment.
- Your parent may be required to pay a gift tax on the value of any joint tenancy over $10,000 when you are named as joint tenant.
- If you should ever go into bankruptcy, your interest in your parent's home can be sold.
- If you ever divorce, your spouse may be entitled to your joint tenancy share.
- When the property is passed to you upon your parent's death, you may have to pay a substantial tax.

Wills.   George's dad laughed when George asked him if he had a will. "What for?" he chuckled. "You and your sister are my only heirs, and I want you two to split everything. There, that's my will. I don't think I need to pay an attorney to write that down!" If only it were as simple as that, George and his sister would have received their rightful inheritance when their father died just a few months later. But the law does not see things as simply as George's dad did. Without a valid, written will, the estate went into probate, and after a lengthy and rather expensive court process, the state took 37 percent of the value of the estate for taxes and left George and his sister arguing over who was responsible for paying for their father's debts and funeral expenses with what was left.

The will is the most common method of formal estate planning. A will is a legally enforceable, written declaration of a person's intended distribution of property after death. After the death of the holder, the will is taken to court, where a probate judge determines its validity and distributes the assets. But it has its drawbacks.

Probate is one reason many families decide not to rely solely on a will to distribute their estate. Probate is a legal process whereby the property of someone who dies is distributed. First, all debts and taxes are paid; the balance of the estate is then distributed to the beneficiaries as designated by the will. In most states this is a simple procedure, but in other states and for larger estates, especially when a valid will does not exist, the probate process can be drawn out over years, tying up all the assets in the estate and resulting in considerable legal fees.

You might say: "Gee, Dad, I know you've made out a will to make sure that your assets go to your family. But I was just reading an article that explained why a will might not be the best way to leave assets to your family. It said something about the fact that all wills have to go through probate, which in some states can cost a lot and take a long time. It said that money over a certain amount bequeathed in a will is open to heavy taxation, and it said that wills don't name the beneficiaries of your life insurance policies and your retirement plan. I was wondering if you were aware of these things?"

This is not to say that your parents don't need a valid will. Even if an estate planner helps your parents move the bulk of their assets into a more protected plan, a will is still necessary to control the distribution of all other monies and possessions, as well as to name an executor of the estate and to designate what monies should be used to pay debts.

A will is relatively inexpensive to prepare with legal counsel. But still some seniors want to write their own will. "Why should I pay somebody to tell me how to distribute my own property?" they reason. But each state has very specific rules and regulations for writing a will, and failure to adhere to one of those stipulations can make the whole will invalid. In many states, a holographic will (a will that is written out in your own handwriting) is automatically invalidated.

The legal fee for this service varies from place to place but is not especially expensive, averaging about $150 (going up to $1,500 or more for more complicated estates). Many older adults can have their wills drawn up for free by their state senior legal services office, or for a very minimal fee by a private lawyer associated with the senior legal services office. Call your Area Agency on Aging for the telephone number of the nearest senior legal services office.

You might say: "Mom and Dad, you have both worked hard to buy your home, gather some savings, and collect possessions that mean a lot to you. And I know it's important to you that these things stay in the family after your death (which we're all assuming won't be for another fifty years!). But I'm worried that the will you both wrote together won't be enough to carry out your wishes. Those preprinted, fill-in-the-blank forms you bought at the stationery store are unlikely to meet your individual needs and circumstances, and may be of little or no value when the will goes to probate court. Why don't you call this financial adviser I know who can help you draw up a real, legal will that will make sure your wishes are carried out?"

Trusts.   A trust allows your parents to share their wealth with the family or favorite charity while still retaining control of the assets and reducing the tax burden. There are several different types of trust that serve different purposes, but they fall into two main categories: living trusts and testamentary trusts.

If your parents set up a trust during their lifetime, called a *living trust*, they transfer any or all stocks, bonds, real estate, savings, and so on into a fund. This trust can be *revocable*, meaning that it can be changed at any time and that the assets are available to your parents at any time. (Revocable trusts are protected from probate but not from taxes.) Or the trust can be *irrevocable*, meaning that it cannot be changed or terminated once it is established and that the assets cannot be withdrawn by your parents. (Irrevocable trusts are protected from both probate and taxes.)

The trust removes assets from the estate and, in the process, significantly reduces the tax load. Your parents would be taxed only on the portion of the assets that is transferred to them during the year. After their death, these assets in trust don't need to go through probate because legally they belong to the trust, not your parents.

There are several general advantages of a living trust:

- It speeds up the distribution of the assets after the death of the holder.
- No one may contest the wishes of the deceased regarding the disposition of the estate.
- The assets within the trust are not open to public scrutiny.
- It may be changed at any time.

- Because the trust avoids probate, the administrative process is less expensive for the heirs, and the lengthy delays often associated with probate are eliminated.

A trust can also protect the assets from the debts of the heirs. If you are a professional who might be sued—a physician or architect, for example—it might be better if your parents set up a trust for you that you can use when you need it and can in turn pass on to your children tax free but that is also protected from any creditors or predators in lawsuits or divorces.

The second basic type of trust, the *testamentary trust*, is established after your parents' death by the terms of their will. Your parent must die before the trust goes into effect. The assets first go through probate upon death and are then placed in the trust. This trust is open to the public for review during the initial estate settlement phase. Any subsequent financial activities that need court approval will also be open to the public. These include various investment activities, income generated from the trust, purchases, sales, and other activities related to the trust estate. If privacy is an issue for your parents, a testamentary trust is not a good option.

You might say: "Mom, you and Dad worked hard for your money, and I know you've been very generous to me and my family in your will, but I've recently read something that I thought we might talk about. If the money is given directly to me, it can be heavily taxed and will be unprotected from my debts. If I should divorce or if I should be sued because of my business or an accident or something, that money could be used as part of any settlement. But if you put that money in a trust for me, I can have access to the money if I need it, but it is protected. Have you ever looked into that?"

A *word of caution:* if your parents are of modest means and do not have valuable assets to pass on after their death, they more than likely do not need to hire an estate planner and prepare trust funds. They probably will not have a costly or lengthy probate in any event, and the effect of settling their estate would be the same with or without a trust. However, it is not uncommon for seniors to be swindled by high-pressure salespeople who exaggerate the cost of probate and sell high-priced estate planning packages through aggressive promotions. You should be aware that fast-talking con artists are selling costly estate planning services and generically written "living trust" documents to seniors who just don't need them.

Talk About Estate Tax Reduction Strategies. Renee's dad was a retired obstetrician-gynecologist. His wife had died two years ago, and he was now closing down his practice and getting ready to retire. As he was organizing his years of paperwork, he mentioned to Renee that his will was prepared and kept in the strongbox in the hall closet. He wanted her to know that she would be well taken care of and told her that his estate was worth about $10 million. Renee gave her dad a big hug and asked him how much of that he wanted her to have. "Why, all of it of course!" he said. "Well, Dad," said Renee, "then you'd better see a financial adviser. Did you know that according to federal tax laws, when you die and that will goes to probate, the government can take as much as $5 million for taxes?" Her dad was shocked. "That's impossible," he said. "I have a will. I thought the state took money only if there was no will." Lots of people think their money is protected from excessive taxation by a will, but it isn't.

You should talk to your parents about the tax burden on their estate if their assets exceed the limit on tax-free inheritance. If your parent is a single person, he or she can pass $675,000 to heirs tax free. If your parents are a married couple and they have a carefully prepared will, they can pass on $1,350,000 tax free. But any money over these amounts can be taxed at excessively high rates of 37 to 55 percent if the estate is left unprotected. These are big numbers. Let's say your widowed dad's estate is worth $2,075,000 upon his death. If you subtract the allowed $675,000 that can be given tax free, you are left with $1,400,000 that is taxable. The tax burden on this amount is over $600,000! To pay this debt (which must be paid in full within nine months after the death), you may have to sell your parents' real estate and stocks. Surely this is not what they expected would happen to your inheritance.

You may look at these numbers and think, "My parents' assets aren't worth this much; they have nothing to worry about." Perhaps that's true, but their assets may be worth more than you first imagine. Assets include their home, any other real estate, investments, bank accounts, personal property, and life insurance. Saving assets from high taxation is the most common reason people seek professional help from an estate planner. These professionals know many ways to legally protect money from these "death taxes," by using such strategies as gifting, charitable trusts, insurance trusts, private annuities, and family limited partnerships (to name a few).

You might say: "Did you read about that celebrity who died and left his family $800 million? I'll bet he had that money in all kinds of trusts and things to avoid giving half of it to the state in taxes. Do you have your money protected from these so-called death taxes?"

You might say: "Did you know that even if you have a will, the government can take 37 to 55 percent of your assets in taxes after your death if those assets are valued over a certain amount? Do you think that will happen to your assets after your death?"

Talk About Power of Attorney. As mentioned earlier, it is absolutely vital to have conversations with your parents about their estate planning while they are of sound body and mind. This is also the time to talk to them about who they would like to have power of attorney for them if there should ever come a time when they cannot make important decisions for themselves.

Aron discovered too late the value of talking about estate planning when parents are of sound body and mind. Aron's dad, Bert, gave him power of attorney several years ago "just in case," though of course Aron hoped he would never have to use it. But then Bert had a stroke that left him in a coma, and that's when Aron found out that the legal paper giving him power of attorney over his father's affairs was useless to him. When Aron tried to access his father's bank account to pay his father's medical bills, he found out that this regular power of attorney gave him limited authority and became void in the event his father became incapacitated. What Aron needed was a durable power of attorney that would let him help Bert when he was unable to make decisions and care for his finances by himself.

Designating a durable power of attorney is a very important aspect of financial planning. It indicates the person who is legally permitted to make legal and financial decisions on the behalf of another even when that person is incapacitated. Without a previously designated durable power of attorney, the family must go through an expensive court ordeal to be granted that power of attorney once the elderly parent becomes mentally or physically incapacitated.

You might say: "Remember when Uncle Phil was in the hospital for so long? Did anyone in his family have power of attorney to take care of his affairs? I guess that's something a lot of people don't think about until it's too late, and then the state has to appoint someone. Do you have a designated power of attorney?"

Talk About Finding an Estate Planner.   As we have discussed, the laws regarding estate planning are complicated, and they change from state to state. If your parents decide to see an estate planner, encourage them to find someone who is legitimate and experienced. You might steer them to a major financial institution that has a recognizable name and reputation. Call your bank, your stock broker, or your financial adviser and ask for a referral to an estate planner. Although the family lawyer may agree that estate planning is a good idea, he or she may not be experienced in this area but can probably give you a referral to an attorney who is.

When contacting agents, your parents should feel free to ask them questions that focus on these four areas:

1. Their education (law school), experience, licenses, credentials, and professional designations
2. Any disciplinary actions that have been taken against them
3. The method of compensation
4. A list of client references

You might say: "Mom and Dad, I just read this story in the paper that said some senior citizens are being pressured by unscrupulous salespeople to buy estate planning packages they really don't need. I think estate planning is a good idea and something you two should look into, but if you do, be very careful about who you choose as your estate planner. It should be someone who works with a reputable company and has lots of experience in this field. And you should take your time to ask questions until you're sure you've found the plan that's best for you."

It's been said that there are only two things you can count on in life: death and taxes. Because there's some truth in that, it is crucial that you talk to your parents about estate planning.

RESOURCE

National Academy of Elder Law Attorneys
(602) 881-4005

This organization provides referrals of attorneys who specialize in estate planning.

EXPERT HELP

This chapter was prepared with the expert help of Gary Katz, a wealth preservation planning specialist with Sagemark Consulting, a division of the Lincoln Financial Group in New Jersey. Katz works with many senior citizens to help them determine the type of estate plan that best fits their needs.

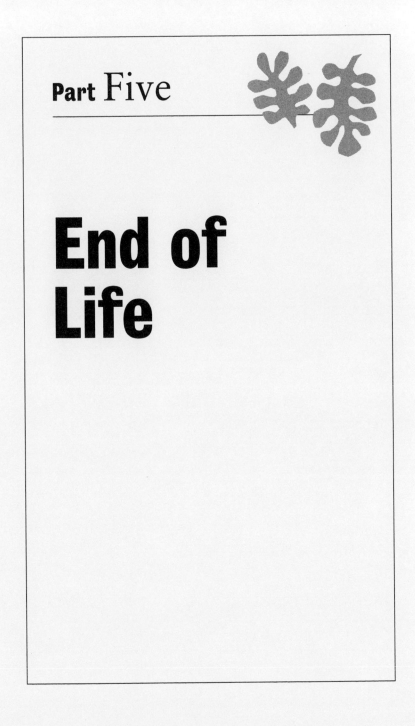

Part Five

End of Life

Funeral Arrangements

Older people are more comfortable talking about their own funeral arrangements than are their children.

> *Joe Weigel, director of marketing*
> *and corporate communications for*
> *Hillenbrand Industries' Funeral Services*

When Rob met his brother, Peter, at noon, he grabbed him in a bear hug and cried. Their mom had died a year ago, and now their dad was gone too. Together both brothers mourned their father's death and then somberly sat down to decide how the final details would be handled.

By three o'clock they were screaming at each other. Rob wanted to use the funeral home in his dad's hometown so old friends could easily visit. Peter wanted to use the funeral home owned by his wife's uncle, who would give them a very good deal. Rob wanted to have a funeral mass in the church; Peter wanted to skip the ceremonies because their dad hadn't been in any church in the last twenty years. Rob wanted a two-night wake; Peter wanted one night. Rob wanted to rent a room at a local restaurant to gather after the burial; Peter refused to help pay for a "party."

Rob and Peter fought for hours over every detail of their father's wake, funeral, and burial. Time that should have been spent giving each other comfort and support was wasted in anger. Obviously, this emotionally painful scene (which is carried out every day all over the country by battling siblings) could have been avoided completely if Rob and Peter had just asked their dad while he was still alive what he wanted them do after his death.

There's no way around it: the only one way to know how your parent wants her funeral conducted is to ask her. Only she can answer the many questions that, if left unanswered, easily become a source of conflict and confusion at the time of death. Although you might feel awkward bringing up the subject, elderly people usually feel comforted by this kind of discussion, knowing that they will not be leaving behind unresolved problems.

This chapter helps you prepare to talk to your parent about the sensitive subject of funeral arrangements. You'll see why it's so important to have this conversation, when the best time is to bring up the subject, and exactly what you might say.

WHY TALK ABOUT FUNERAL ARRANGEMENTS

You should talk to your parent about his funeral arrangements because, like every other major life event, death should be discussed and prepared for in advance. Would you ever consider waiting until the day before your wedding or the birth of your child to discuss such details as where the event will take place and who will pay for it? Of course not. Yet too many people wait until the death of a parent to think about the details of the funeral and burial.

Talking to your parent about her funeral arrangements will not make her feel discarded or old—it will make her feel content and at ease knowing that she has made her wishes known. "If she wants to make her wishes known," you might wonder, "why doesn't she just tell me?" The truth is, she may want to but feels too embarrassed to say, "I want the announcement of my death in these three newspapers, and I want to wear the blue dress that your father always liked." She may also feel that you are uncomfortable talking about her death, and assumes that if she were to bring up the subject you would say something like, "Oh don't talk like that. You're not dying." By asking her what she wants, you give her permission to talk about these things, which she has probably thought about in great detail but didn't know how to tell you.

You should also talk to your parent about his funeral arrangements to make it easier on yourself. When the funeral director sat down with Daniel to map out the plans for his father's funeral, Daniel was not only grief-stricken; he felt like a negligent fool as well. He couldn't answer any of the simple questions he was asked. He assumed his father wanted to be buried in the same plot with his mother, but to be honest, he hadn't been there in years and couldn't remember the name of the cemetery or even the town it was in. Nor did he know the name of his father's synagogue. He remembered his father talking about the rabbi and his friends in the congregation, but he had no idea where the synagogue was. He did know that his father would rather have his friends donate money to a charity in his name rather than send flowers, but he had no idea what charity his father especially liked. Daniel was embarrassed and ashamed that he knew so little about his father's life, but when he had phoned him every Sunday evening they never talked about these things. There was so much to find out in a hurry; Daniel prayed he wouldn't make any major mistakes.

Although it may seem selfish, it is nevertheless true that you should talk to your parent about her funeral arrangements for your own sake as well as hers, for several reasons. Talking in advance about funeral arrangements

- Reduces a lot of anxiety around decision making at the time of death, when you're not emotionally able to make intelligent decisions
- Reduces the likelihood of paying for an excessively expensive funeral out of remorse rather than out of real desire or need
- Prevents sibling warfare over the "right" way
- Gives you confidence and peace of mind because you know exactly what your parent wants

There is one last reason you should talk to your parent about his funeral. Letting him dictate the details of this important event can be an empowering experience—if you let him make his own decisions. When you talk about this subject, let your parent hear "Tell me what you want" rather than "Don't worry; I'll take care of it."

WHEN TO TALK ABOUT FUNERAL ARRANGEMENTS

Conversations about funerals in general can happen anytime. But when you really want to get the facts straight, try to do it with the following four points discussed in this section in mind. Talk to your parent when

- Your parent is critically ill—if you must
- Your parent is healthy
- All siblings are present
- You're prepared to talk in detail

When Your Parent Is Critically Ill—If You Must

If your parent is critically ill and you haven't yet talked about funeral arrangements, you may find yourself faced with the necessity of a deathbed conversation about this emotional subject. Of course you may be tempted to avoid the topic of funerals at this time and say instead, "Don't worry, Dad. You're going to be just fine." But most critically ill people know their time on earth is nearly over and would be happy if someone would help them make their funeral arrangements.

If your dying parent does not bring up the subject, don't assume he doesn't want to talk about his death. He may be trying to spare you the pain of this conversation. Although the circumstances of a deathbed discussion will make it difficult for you to think of all the details you need to cover, and your parent will not able to think clearly about what he really wants, these "last-minute" talks are better than nothing. Don't be afraid to bring up the subject; then take your parent's response as your cue about whether or not to continue.

When Your Parent Is Healthy

The best time to talk about funeral arrangements is when your parents are still quite healthy in body and mind and able to think carefully about what they would like. If you wait until they are ill, you invite misunderstandings and hurt feelings.

When talking about this subject, timing is very important. Let's say your mom suffers a minor stroke. As you dash off to meet her in the emergency room, this minicrisis makes you realize that your mom is getting older and that one of these times an attack may be fatal. You make a mental note to talk to her about what funeral arrangements she would like. Later, as you're sitting with your mom waiting for her doctor to discharge her from the hospital, you strike up a conversation that begins, "Mom, what funeral home do you like?" Your mom will have one of two reactions: she'll think you're getting ready to put her in the grave before it's really time to go, or she'll think she's more critically ill than anybody is telling her. In this situation, the timing of this question creates feelings of anger and fear rather than empowerment. The conversation is bound to go much better if you choose a time when your parent is quite healthy and able to think carefully about her answers.

When All Siblings Are Present

Caron remembers how upset she was during her mother's funeral because her brother and sister would not believe that their mother wanted to be cremated. "I swear," Caron pleaded, "Mom told me that's what she wanted." Well, unfortunately Mom never told anyone else, and because it was two against one, the body was embalmed and buried. "I still feel kind of guilty that I didn't carry out her wish," says Caron. "It never occurred to me to tell my brother and sister about Mom's request before she died; I just figured it would be no problem—boy, was I wrong."

When you talk to your parents about how they want their funeral arrangements handled, it's a very good idea to have your siblings present (assuming you have siblings). Having at the very least one other who can "witness" the conversation avoids the common argument at the time of death over what "Mom told me" but didn't tell anyone else.

It's not necessary or usual for an adult child to call all family members together for the sole purpose of discussing funeral arrangements of a perfectly healthy parent. Instead, you should bring up the subject very matter-of-factly at a simple family gathering—say a birthday party or backyard barbecue.

Depending on your family relationships and dynamics, you can talk to your siblings first and approach your parents as a team.

You might say: "Mom and Dad, we were thinking that while we're all together like this it might be a good idea to find out how you two want your funeral arrangements handled when you die fifty years from now. Suzy says she'll be our secretary and write it all down so there'll be no mistakes."

Keep the tone upbeat and positive. This isn't a farewell address; it's the conversation of a family joined together to work out the details of an event that is inevitable for everybody.

Another approach is to tell your parents first that you would like to talk to them about their funeral plans and to enlist their help in getting your siblings to gather round the table.

You might say: "Mom and Dad, I was thinking that it's not that often we all get together, so this might be a good chance while you're both in good health to sit down and talk about the things you want us to know about your funeral plans. That way we'll have everything mapped out and we'll be able to carry out your wishes without any disagreements. How about after dinner? Will you call everyone in to sit down or shall I?"

You know what would work best in your particular family. The goal is to have all siblings know exactly what your parents want.

When You're Prepared to Talk in Detail

When you bring up the subject of funeral arrangements, be prepared to talk in detail. Unlike some of the other topics we've discussed in this book—such as money management, consumer fraud, and grief support, which should be subjects of many discussions—talking about funeral arrangements is usually a one-time conversation. It's awkward to go back to your parents a year after your first discussion and say, "I forget: What was it you wanted for your funeral?" or "Do you still want to be cremated?" You probably will discuss the details of the funeral only once, so be sure to cover all the bases.

Know in advance what questions you want to ask, and jot down your parents' answers. Then store the paper in a place that you'll be able to easily find upon their death.

WHAT YOU SHOULD TALK ABOUT

You will probably open up your conversation about funeral arrangements talking about general topics, other people and their funerals, and what your own parents may prefer. Then you'll progress to the nitty-gritty details. Take it one step at a time and give your folks time to think. Like a wedding, this is an expensive passage and lots of people will be there—there's no reason to rush the details.

Breaking the Ice

To broach the subject of funeral arrangements, you can use opportunities that arise around the death of a friend or family member, or even that of a public figure in the news.

If you yourself go to a funeral, you might talk about the details in general conversation. Talk about the flowers, then ask your parents what they think about obituaries that ask friends to donate to a particular charity rather than send flowers. Talk about the family's decision to have the person cremated, then ask your parents if they know anyone who was cremated and what they think of that. Talking about someone else's funeral is an easy way to ease into this conversation.

You might say: "Dad, I went to Jake's father's wake last night. I was surprised that they had a closed casket. I wonder why?"

After your parent goes to a funeral, she may make a remark about the way the funeral was run, or you can ask how the ceremony was conducted. This is a good time to seize the moment and be a bit more direct.

You might say: "Have you ever thought about how you'd like us to take care of your funeral?"

If one parent has already died, you might casually reminisce about that funeral at a family gathering.

You might say: "I remember so much about the day of Dad's funeral. Remember that beautiful eulogy Uncle Gary gave? Mom, do you think that funeral went well? Are there any details that you would like handled differently at your funeral?"

It is easy to open the door to this subject if you talk first about somebody else's funeral and then bring the focus back home.

Addressing Specific Issues

Once you get a conversation going about funerals in general, steer the discussion to the specifics of your parent's funeral.

You might say: "We're hoping we won't need to know your feelings about funeral arrangements for another 120 years, but when that time comes, we want to make sure we do what you want."

Then ask your parent questions about what he prefers regarding all the arrangements. You might use the following checklist to identify the details that match your family, cultural, and religious needs.

If we have a choice, do you want to have an autopsy performed?

What would you like to include in your obituary? What papers would you like us to contact?

Where do you want to have your funeral? (In the state where you have retired or in your "home" state?)

What funeral home do you want to use?

Do you want to be cremated, embalmed, or buried but not embalmed?

Do you want a wake? How many nights? Open or closed casket?

Do you have any special outfit you'd like to be buried in?

What kind of memorial service do you want? Where do you want it? Do you want to have any readings or songs that you especially like?

Are there people you would want me to notify about your death that I might not think of?

(If your parent wants to be buried) What kind of casket do you want? (Top of the line or more moderately priced?)

Where do you want to be buried? Below ground or in a mausoleum?

Do you want to be buried with your wedding and engagement rings on, or do you want to have them removed and kept by the family as heirlooms?

Do you have any preference about who your pallbearers might be?

Do you want to be an organ donor?

Your goal in asking these questions is to find out what things are important to your parents so that you can carry out their wishes. There may be some things they feel very strongly about, others that they will leave to your discretion, and still others that they need to think about and discuss with you at another time. If your parent should say, "Oh, I don't care. Do what you think is best," don't push the matter.

You might say: "Well, I just want to do what you would like, so if you think of anything, be sure to tell me. Think about the wake, the memorial service, the burial, or even the family gathering afterwards. Just let me know if there is anything special you want."

EXPERT HELP

This chapter was written with the expert help of Joe Weigel, director of marketing and corporate communications for Hillenbrand Industries' Funeral Services Group, headquartered in Batesville, Indiana.

Chapter Notes

Driving Safety

Eberhand, J. W. "Safe Mobility for Senior Citizens." *IATSS Research*, 1996, 20(1), 29–37.

Insurance Institute for Highway Safety. *Facts, 1996 Fatalities: Elderly*. Arlington, Va.: Insurance Institute for Highway Safety, 1997.

Spreitzer-Berent, B. "Supporting the Mature Driver." Royal Oak, Mich.: AgeQuest, 1999.

Transportation Research Board, National Research Council. *Transportation in an Aging Society: Improving Mobility for Older Persons*. Special Report 218, Vol. 1. Washington, D.C.: Transportation Research Board, 1988.

Late-Onset Alcoholism

"How to Talk to an Older Person Who Has a Problem with Alcohol or Medications." *The Responsibility of Friendship*. West Palm Beach, Fla.: Hazelden Publishing and Education, n.d.

Late-Life Romance

American Association of Retired Persons. "A Profile of Older Americans 1997." [http://research.aarp.org/general/profile97.html#marital]. December 1996.

Padawer, R. "Lovers over Fifty-Five Embracing Cohabitation." *The Record*, July 17, 2000, pp. 1, 5.

Geriatric Care Managers
Federal Trade Commission and the American Association of Retired Persons. "Selecting a Geriatric Care Manager." *Aging/Parents & Adult Children Together*, n.d.

Grief and Bereavement
Kübler-Ross, E. *On Death and Dying*. New York: Simon & Schuster, 1997.

Depression
Billig, N. *To Be Old and Sad*. San Francisco: Jossey-Bass, 1987.

Castleman, M. "Coping with Depression: Depression in Elderly People." [http://www.depression.com/tools/health_library/coping/elderly.html]. May 2000.

Diagnostic and Statistical Manual of Mental Disorders. (4th ed.) Washington, D.C.: American Psychiatric Association, 1994.

Mathiasen, P., and Levert, S. *Late Life Depression*. New York: Dell, 1997.

Dementia
FCA Clearinghouse. "Factsheets: Dementia." [http://www.caregiver.org]. July 1996.

National Library of Medicine. "Dementia." [http://text.nlm.nih.gov]. September 27, 2000.

Choosing to Live at Home
Federal Trade Commission and American Association of Retired Persons. "Making the Home Senior Friendly." *Aging/Parents & Adult Children Together*, n.d.

National Association for Home Care. "Home- and Community-Based Services." *Homecare Agency Locator*. [http://www.nahc.org] n.d.

Alternative Living Arrangements

National Institutes of Health. *Aging America Poses Unprecedented Challenge, Says New Census, Aging Institute Report.* [http://www.nih.gov/nia/new/press/census.htm]. May 20, 1996.

General Information Resources

Area Agencies on Aging
The Older Americans Act provides federal money so states can operate programs for people age sixty and older. The State Agencies on Aging distribute the money to local Area Agencies on Aging (AAAs). They oversee a complex, statewide service system and provide policy direction and technical assistance to the AAAs within their states. The AAAs can be of tremendous assistance to those providing or seeking elder care services. They are advocates for older people and provide a comprehensive array of home and community services such as transportation, home-delivered meals, legal services, publications, and crisis response. Many of the services available through AAAs are free or based on a person's ability to pay.

For information about Older Americans Act programs, contact the Eldercare Locator at (800) 677-1116 or check out the website of the National Association of Area Agencies on Aging at www.n4a.org.

Other Useful Contacts

Administration on Aging
330 Independence Avenue SW
Washington, DC 20201
(202) 619-7501
www.aoa.gov

Alzheimer's Association
919 North Michigan Avenue, Suite 1000
Chicago, IL 60611
(800) 272-3900
www.alz.org

Alzheimer's Disease Education and Referral Center
P.O. Box 8250
Silver Spring, MD 20907
(800) 438-4380
www.alzheimers.org
adear@alzheimers.org (e-mail)

American Association of Homes and Services for the Aging
901 E Street NW
Washington, DC 20004
(202) 783-2242
(800) 508-9442
www.aahsa.org

American Association of Retired Persons (AARP)
601 E Street NW
Washington, DC 20049
(800) 424-3410
www.aarp.org

Eldercare Locator
(800) 677-1116 (weekdays 9 A.M. to 8 P.M. EST)
www.aoa.gov/elderpage/locator.html

The Eldercare Locator is a nationwide directory assistance service
that helps older persons and their caregivers find help locally.

National Association for Home Care
228 Seventh Street SE
Washington, DC 20003
(202) 547-7424
www.nahc.org

National Council on the Aging
409 Third Street SW, Suite 200
Washington, DC 20024
(202) 479-1200
www.ncoa.org

The National Institute on Aging
P.O. Box 8057
Gaithersburg, MD 20898-8057
(800) 222-2225, TTY (800) 222-4225

Government-Sponsored Online Sites
Access America for Seniors
www.seniors.gov

This is a federal interagency website offering consumer
information from nineteen government agencies.

Administration on Aging
www.aoa.gov

This website has links to many sites of interest to senior citizens, addressing topics such as health, finances, insurance, long-term care, and legal issues.
www.hcfa.gov

Health Care Financing Administration
www.hcfa.gov

This office oversees the operations of the Medicare and Medicaid programs. For comparisons of Medicare and Medigap policies, go to www.medicare.gov.

Social Security Administration
www.ssa.gov

This site shows you everything about Social Security and its many services.

Other Recommended Online Sites for Seniors
Age of Reason: www.ageofreason.com
Eldercare Web: www.elderweb.com
ElderNet: www.eldernet.com
Go60.Com: www.go60.com
Interactive Aging Network: www.ianet.org
National Senior Citizens Law Center: www.nscic.org
Online Guide to Retirement Living: www.retirement-living.com
Retire.net: www.retire.net
Senior Sites: www.seniorsites.com
ThirdAge.Com: www.thirdage.com
Widownet: www.widownet.com

The Author

Theresa Foy DiGeronimo, M.Ed., is adjunct professor of English at The William Paterson University of New Jersey and the mother of three children. She is the coauthor of *How to Talk to Your Kids About Really Important Things, How to Talk to Teens About Really Important Things, Keeping Your Kids Out Front Without Kicking Them from Behind,* and dozens of other parenting and children's books. She lives in Hawthorne, New Jersey.